S0-AYP-760

ACT ESSAY PRACTICE

Write Here, Write Now!

LEARNING EXPRESS ®

NEW YORK

Nokomis Public Library

Copyright © 2007 LearningExpress, LLC.

All rights reserved under International and Pan-American Copyright Conventions.
Published in the United States by LearningExpress, LLC, New York.

Library of Congress Cataloging-in-Publication Data:
   ACT essay practice : write here, write now!
      p. cm.
   ISBN: 978-1-57685-591-1
   1. ACT Assessment—Study guides. 2. English language—Composition and
exercises—Examinations—Study guides.
LB2353.48.A276 2007
378.1'662—dc22

              2007009008

Printed in the United States of America

9 8 7 6 5 4 3 2 1

ISBN: 978-1-57685-591-1

For information on LearningExpress, other LearningExpress products, or bulk sales,
please write to us at:
   55 Broadway
   8th Floor
   New York, NY 10006

Or visit us at:
   www.learnatest.com

ACT ESSAY PRACTICE

Write Here, Write Now!

DISCARD

About the Contributor

Tamra Orr is a full-time educational writer living in the Pacific Northwest. She has written several test-prep books and works for a dozen of the nation's largest testing companies. She is the author of more than 70 books, mom to four, and wife to one.

Contents

Learn What You Need to Know before You Actually Need to Know It

Lucky you! You're getting ready to take the ACT. (Yes, I am psychic . . . no, not really, but if you picked up this book, then that was a pretty solid guess.) If you thought that ACT meant you got to go up on stage and act, sing, or dance until you were given an Academy Award, you picked up the wrong book. The ACT is actually a test that you take during your high school years. It is very similar to the SAT. Both exams are designed to test you on everything you have learned since you were born (okay, not quite) and to help you get into the college(s) of your choice (ideally). The good news is that the ACT has only four multiple-choice sections (compared to SAT's ten!)—Math, Science, Reading, and English. The additional Writing Test measures how well you can plan and write a short essay.

Because nothing is scarier than facing the unknown, let's take a minute to learn more about the test before you blindly panic, leave the country, clone yourself so the clone can take the test, or give up before you begin and do nothing to prepare yourself.

▶ Numbers, Numbers

The test is about three-and-a-half hours (not including short breaks), and in that amount of time, you get to chance to answer 216 questions, which are broken down as follows:

SUBJECT	NUMBER OF QUESTIONS	TIME LIMIT
English	75	45 minutes
Math	60	60 minutes
Reading	40	35 minutes
Science	40	35 minutes
Writing	1	30 minutes

Now, the big news: The ACT Writing Test is optional. That's right. You don't have to take it.

Optional—Not Really

WAIT! I know what you're about to do. You're getting ready to put this back on the shelf and go check out the latest manga book in the graphic novel section. Well, forget it. Just because that essay is optional doesn't mean it's a free ticket for you to leave early. You *are* going to take that part of the test—and here's why.

The Top Ten List of Reasons Why You Are Going to Take the (Optional) ACT Writing Test

10. You are an opinionated person by nature and you look forward to any opportunity to write about your point on view on an issue.
9. You enjoy challenging yourself and this is a real challenge!
8. You will make your mom, dad, grandma, grandpa, and even the dog so proud.
7. This book fits so nicely in your backpack.
6. You can brag to your friends that you are so confident in your intellectual abilities that you even took part of the test that you didn't have to!
5. You will be proud of yourself for being one of the tough students who took it all!
4. Colleges often use this score to help know where to place you in first-year classes.
3. Colleges also often use this writing score to help you pinpoint a potential major.
2. High ACT scores can help you obtain additional scholarships.

And the number-one reason . . .

1. Many colleges (approximately 75% of them, in fact) expect you to have taken that writing test. If you haven't and they require it, you're out!

So, as you can see, there are some pretty convincing reasons. (If you still aren't completely persuaded, though, please reread number 1.)

What else do you need to know about this test? Let's look at how it's scored, fees, and registration, and finally, we will focus on the point of this whole book—getting ready for that ACT essay.

► Scores, Scores, and More Scores

The ACT is scored much differently from the SAT. With the ACT, there is no penalty for a wrong answer. You just do not get a point for it. You also do not get a point for anything you leave blank. This should be a huge clue to you not to leave a single question blank if you can help it. At least a guess gives you a chance of getting it right. Even picking answers that make a pretty pattern on the page is better than leaving things blank.

The way the ACT reviewers arrive at your test scores is more complicated than just adding up your correct answers. First, they take the number of correct answers and convert them to scaled scores, which allow each test, regardless of the number of questions, to have the same range. Each one of the four multiple-choice sections of the test is scored with a range between 1 (the lowest) and 36 (the highest). All four scores (one from each section) are added together and then averaged to get your composite score. If you got a 30 in Math, 28 in English, 24 in Science, and 22 in Reading, you would have an average score of 26. (Add all four scores together and divide by four.) You will also get a percentage score, which will show you where you compare with other students in your state and in the entire nation. The higher that percentage is, the better your score.

If you take the optional Writing Test, you will receive two additional scores beyond what you would receive if you took only the ACT multiple-choice tests. You must take both the English and Writing Tests to receive writing scores. You will receive a Writing Test subscore and a combined English-writing score, plus comments about your essay.

The combined English/Writing Test score is created by using a formula that weighs the English Test score as two-thirds of the total and the Writing Test score as one-third of the total to form a combined score. This combined score is reported on a 1–36 scale: 1 being the lowest and 36 being the highest.

	6 Effective Skill	5 Competent Skill	4 Adequate Skill	3 Developing Skill	2 Inconsistent/ Weak Skill	1 Little/No Skill
Understanding of task	excellent and insightful understanding of assignment; provides critical context for discussion of issue; shows insight into complexities of issue; provides counterarguments	good understanding of assignment; provides broad context for discussion of issue; shows some insight into complexities of issue; provides some counterarguments	good understanding of assignment with some context for discussion of issue; shows recognition of complexities of issue and counterarguments	basic understanding of assignment; takes a clear position; shows some recognition of complexities of issue and counterarguments	weak understanding of assignment; does not take a clear position on issue; shows little recognition of complexities of issue and counterarguments	little to no understanding of assignment; position on issue is not clear or nonexistent
Development of argument	well developed with specific and interesting examples	adequately developed with specific and appropriate examples	some development with some specific examples	little development; tends to be very general	lack of development; inappropriate examples	complete lack of development; examples are either nonexistent or completely off topic
Organization of essay	clear pattern of organization; uses clear logic and excellent transitions between ideas	generally well organized; uses clear logic with good transitions between ideas	organized with some inconsistencies; uses recognizable logic with some transitions between ideas	inconsistent organization; uses some logic with a few transitions between ideas	disorganized; logic is difficult to follow, and there are few transitions between ideas	no attempt at organization; argument is illogical and/or disorganized; there are few or no transitions between ideas
Language/Style/ Mechanics (grammar, spelling, punctuation, etc.)	excellent command of written language with varied sentence structure and sophisticated vocabulary	good command of written English with attempts at varying sentence structure and attempts at sophisticated vocabulary use	adequate command of written language with some minor errors; little sentence variety and only basic vocabulary	noticeable errors in grammar; little or no attempt at sentence variety	many errors in grammar, making comprehension difficult	many errors in grammar, making comprehension extremely difficult

Two trained readers score your essay holistically, giving it a rating from 1–6 (1 being the lowest; 6 being the highest). This means that each scorer assigns an overall score that he or she thinks best represents the entire essay, taking all the aspects of writing into account: understanding of the prompt, development of the writer's ideas, organization of those ideas, and skills in language use. The sum of these readers' ratings is your Writing Test subscore, which can range from 2–12 (2 being the lowest; 12 being the highest).

Your trained readers are usually former or retired English teachers or professional test readers. If their scores vary by more than one point (i.e., one gave it a 3 and the other a 5), a third reader is asked to read your essay to decide the final score.

The essay rating from 1–6 is based on the modified ACT rubric (scoring guide) on page xii.

It is also important for you to realize a few things about the people reading your essay. Although you may imagine them thoughtfully pursing their lips, leaning back slowly in a chair, giving your opinion some heavy consideration, and cheering on your strongest points and tsk-tsking your weaker ones with a sense of disappointment, it's not an accurate picture. The average essay reader spends two minutes or fewer on your essay. Yes, I know. Two minutes is not much time at all considering how much thought you put into each one of those words, but it is the truth. Your reader typically reads the essay *quickly* and then scores it holistically. A reader simply doesn't have time for any more. There's a pile of 300 more essays sitting on the desk waiting to be read and scored. Does this mean the reader doesn't really pay attention to your essay? No. It means that he or she is an expert who understands the elements of a good or bad essay and can quickly assess their presence or absence in an essay. Make your essay as easy to score as possible. Write clearly. Write precisely. Make your point and support it.

► Invest in Yourself

Don't stop reading now—there is *more* good news for you. You not only get to choose whether or not to take the test, but you also get to invest in the opportunity. It's true! The 2006–2007 basic fee for the ACT with the Writing Test is $43. (The basic fee for the ACT if you don't take the Writing Test is $29—$14 less.)

Keep in mind that if you register late or change the date of your exam, there is a penalty. Your scores will automatically be sent to the four colleges you list on your application; if you want them sent to more schools than that, the charge is $8 per additional college you list. It takes four to seven weeks to get your scores, but if you simply cannot wait that long, you can pay an extra $8 and view them on the Internet sooner.

▶ Probing the Prompt

The writing prompt you are given for your essay will be a secret until you open your test booklet. You may have already spent some years developing strong opinions and are ready to defend your point of view to anyone who disagrees with you. Right now, those traits will help you out!

The prompts on the ACT are designed to present an issue that is important to high school or college students—you! The issue always has two sides, which are both presented in the prompt. The trained readers are not really interested in which side you argue. They are interested in the *quality* of your argument.

Before you even start thinking about ideas to put in your essay, you should make sure you understand the prompt and what is being asked of you. Let's take a closer look at a sample prompt and analyze its components:

> The local high school has been under immense pressure to meet high standards as measured by standardized assessment examinations. The scores on these standardized tests have been decreasing in recent years. Some school officials have proposed eliminating physical education classes in order to allow the teachers and students to concentrate more fully on the academic subjects—particularly math and language arts. Supporters of this idea believe that physical education classes are simply a waste of time and effort and that the time and resources could be better used preparing students for standardized tests. Those against this proposal believe that physical education is just as important to students' education as any academic subject.
>
> In your essay, <u>take a position on this issue.</u> You may write about either one of the two points of view given, or you may present a different point of view on this topic. <u>Use specific reasons and examples to support your position.</u>

The prompt can be broken down into three components:

1. The controversial issue

The prompt begins by presenting a controversial issue that the test writers believe is important to high school and college–age students. It might be helpful for you to write a phrase that paraphrases the issue. In this example, the issue could be stated simply as "the elimination of physical education classes."

2. The opposing sides of the issue

The next part of the prompt gives you the two opposing sides of the issue. There is always a side that is *for* the issue and a side that is *against* it. It may be helpful for you to condense the ideas of each side into a phrase or sentence of your own:

> **For:** *will allow more time for academics and better test scores*
> **Against:** *physical education is very important to students' education*

3. Directions for writing

Finally, the prompt gives you directions for writing the essay. This part of the prompt is always the same. The most important aspects of this part are underlined for you in the sample prompt: "take a position on this issue" and "use specific reasons and examples to support your position."

It is very important for you to decide quickly what your position on the issue is. The prompt indicates that you may argue for or against the issue or "present a different point of view." Our advice is that you choose a side that is presented in the prompt and stick with it. It's simply easier and quicker than trying to come up with an entirely different viewpoint on the issue. Additionally, presenting a new viewpoint may cause you to stray off topic. Remember that the new viewpoint must still address the proposed issue. You may be more tempted to stray off the given issue if you try to present a third option.

Usually, you will find yourself reacting emotionally to one side or the other. Even if you don't entirely agree with one side, choose the one you mostly agree with. Once again, it may be helpful for you to jot down your position in a phrase or sentence:

> *I am against eliminating physical education classes.*

You will be given a certain amount of space to write your essay. Remember, those essay readers do not come with automatic word counts built in like your computer does, and even if they did, it wouldn't matter. There is no word count requirement on the essay. Just do your best to fill up the pages. Do not write extra large or skip lines. Most essays that score a 3 or above are more than 250 words and fewer than 400.

This gives you an idea of what kinds of prompts you are going to see on your test. If you get familiar with their format, wording, and style now, it will make test day easier in the long run. That is why this book is here!

HINTS FOR TAKING THE EXAM

- Get a good night's sleep and eat a good meal before the exam.
- Bring all required items (such as writing instruments, identification, and/or a receipt).
- Don't change your mind after making your prompt selection.
- Underline the key words in your prompt.
- Write legibly. You won't get points for neatness, but if readers can't read it, they can't score it.
- Wear a watch, and make a plan for budgeting your time.

▶ So, Now What?

Now that you know what the ACT is and what it will require of you, it's time to focus on the essay and how to use this book.

Part One of the book gives you a broad overview of the grammar you probably learned years ago. Chances are, you've forgotten it, so some reminders are usually needed. The grammar section will be divided into:

- using the mechanics of grammar—punctuation and capitalization
- putting sentences together—using variety and using it correctly
- staying in agreement—a look at making sure verbs, nouns, and pronouns are all in happy agreement
- writing verbs—making sure that you not only keep the same tense throughout, but also choose exciting and expressive ones instead of boring, dull, and overused ones
- including modifiers—adding details that make writing jump off the page and into the reader's mind
- choosing correct diction—using the right words and avoiding the wrong ones

Part Two of this book is a thorough look at how essays are built from the ground up. It will make sure you understand and use:

- the prewriting exercises that make the actual writing easier and smoother
- the ways to write an introduction that states your main point/opinion and grabs the reader's attention
- the techniques that go into creating the strong and supportive middle of the essay—otherwise known as the **body**

- the various ways to end an essay without sounding trite or boring
- the important final touches you need to give your essay before you let it go

Finally, Part Three of the book includes 40 different prompts for you to use as practice for the actual test. Four of those prompts are accompanied by sample written essays, ranging from a 1-point score to a 6-point score, so you can see examples of essays at different scoring levels. They are also followed by reviewer comments, which will show you why the essays earned the scores they did.

So, sit back and get comfy. Put your feet up and prepare to be fascinated, enthralled, and amazed. Pick up this book and start studying!

CONTACTING ACT

If you have any questions about taking the ACT that are not answered here, you should contact ACT directly:

ACT
500 ACT Drive
P.O. Box 168
Iowa City, IA 52243-0168
319-337-1000
www.act.org

ACT ESSAY PRACTICE

Write Here, Write Now!

ONE

Grammar—Up Close and Personal

"Arguments over grammar and style are often as fierce as those over IBM versus Mac and as fruitless as Coke versus Pepsi and boxers versus briefs."

— Jack Lynch

Ready for Some G.U.M.?

Well, if you are sitting there pondering whether you'd prefer spearmint or bubblegum, then once again, I am the bearer of bad news. In this case, G.U.M. doesn't stand for that rubbery stuff that Native Americans discovered and used to stave off hunger. Instead, it stands for **G**rammar, **U**sage, and **M**echanics (G.U.M.). We're going to get in a virtual time-travel machine here and zip back to elementary school when you first learned about capitalization and punctuation. The desks might be too small to sit in now though, so just plop down somewhere more comfortable.

▶ Why Punctuation, Spelling, and Grammar Are so Important

The good news is that your essay will *not* be graded on punctuation or capitalization. How in the world do you think that those readers could do that in your allotted two minutes? So, if there is a comma splice, a mistaken use of the semicolon, or an oops-you-forget-to-capitalize-it word in there, you will not be scored lower. So, what's the point of going over all of this, you ask? There are two answers to that question—one is immediate gratification and the other is delayed gratification.

By using proper punctuation and capitalization, your essay will be easier to read and understand, which you know is important. You want your readers to think, "Wow, this student really knows what he or she is doing," not "What the heck is that supposed to mean?" Capitalization and punctuation are a big part of that. Of course, the delayed gratification part of this is that knowing the basics will help you be a better writer for the rest of high school, on through college, and at work.

So, let's get started by looking at capitalization. Then, we'll turn to punctuation, which includes periods, question marks, exclamation marks, quotation marks, semicolons, colons, apostrophes, and commas.

▶ The Capital of What?

Have you ever wondered why we have capital letters and lowercase letters? I bet that has been a question weighing heavily on your mind for some years now. You can blame the ancient Romans for it. When they began carving everything they could think of on the fronts and sides of buildings, they found out they rather quickly ran out of room. Rather than take a lesson on being too wordy, they decided to make smaller letters. Ta-dah! Uppercase and lowercase letters were born.

Today, of course, capitals are used for many other reasons. How many can you think of right off the top of your head? Go ahead!

_____

_____

_____

Okay, thanks for participating. Now, here are some of the rules when it comes to capitals. I am not including all of them because, while they are important, they do not apply to what you need to know for the essay. For example, openings and closings of letters or a line of poetry involve capitals, but you won't need to use that in your essay.

Capitalization Checklist

✔ The first word of every sentence ➔ *Yes, we do carry the matching bed skirt.*

✔ The first word of a quoted sentence (not just a quoted phrase) ➔ *And with great flourish, he sang, "O beautiful for spacious skies, for amber waves of grain!"*

✔ The specific name of a person (and his or her title), a place, or a thing (otherwise known as *proper nouns*). **Proper nouns** include specific locations and geographic regions; political, social, and athletic organizations and agencies; historical events, documents, and periods; nationalities and their language; religions, their members, and their deities; brand or trade names; and holidays.

✔ The abbreviation for *proper nouns* (Government agencies are probably the most frequently abbreviated. Remember to capitalize each letter.) ➔ *The CIA makes me feel just a little nervous.*

✔ Adjectives (descriptive words) derived from *proper nouns* ➔ *the American* (adjective) *flag*

✔ The pronoun *I*.

✔ The most important words in a title ➔ *Last March, I endured a 24-hour public reading of* Moby Dick.

Never knew there were that many, did you?

CAPITALIZATION RUNS IN THE FAMILY

When writing your ACT essay, avoid unnecessarily capitalizing words referring to family members. Capitalize them only if they are used in place of names. Look at the following examples:

> *Although Aunt Matilda has arrived, my other aunts are late.*
> *After my mother lectured me, Father yelled.*

Look closely at the second example. If a word such as *my, our, your, his, her,* or *their* comes before the word referring to a family member, it is not capitalized. The word *mother* is not capitalized because the word *my* comes before it. However, no such word comes before *Father*. In fact, *Father* is used in place of the man's name, making it a proper name. That's why it's capitalized!

▶ The "Punk" of Grammar . . . Punctuation

I've given this a lot of thought and I don't think there really is a way to make punctuation exciting. It's like taking out the garbage or taking the dog for a walk—an essential part of life that rarely makes the heart beat faster and the adrenaline course through your veins. However, never underestimate the importance of proper punctuation in your essay.

We will cover eight main aspects of punctuation. Yes, there are others like dashes, hyphens, ellipses, and more. But, let's focus on the ones that follow.

Punctuation Checklist

Periods

- ✔ At the end of a declarative sentence (sentences that make a statement) ➔ *Today, I took a walk to nowhere.*
- ✔ At the end of a command or request ➔ *Here's a cloth. Now gently burp the baby on your shoulder.*
- ✔ At the end of an indirect question ➔ *Jane asked if I knew where she had left her keys.*
- ✔ Before a decimal number ➔ *Statisticians claim that the average family raises 2.5 children.*
- ✔ Between dollars and cents ➔ *I remember when $1.50 could buy the coolest stuff.*
- ✔ After an initial in a person's name ➔ *You are Sir James W. Dewault, are you not?*
- ✔ After an abbreviation ➔ *On Jan. 12, I leave for Africa.*

Question Marks

- ✔ At the end of a question ➔ *Why do you look so sad?*
- ✔ Inside a quotation mark when the quote is a question ➔ *She asked, "Why do you look so sad?"*

Exclamation Points

- ✔ At the end of a word, phrase, or sentence filled with emotion ➔ *Oh my God! There is Beyoncé!*
- ✔ Inside a quotation mark when the quote is an exclamation ➔ *The teenage girl screamed, "Oh my God! There is Beyoncé!"*

Quotation Marks

- ✔ When directly quoting dialogue, not when paraphrasing ➔ Hamlet says, *"To be, or not to be. That is the question."*

✔ For titles of chapters, articles, short stories, poems, songs, or periodicals ➔ *My favorite short story is "Flowers for Algernon."*

Semicolons

✔ Between two independent clauses (An **independent clause** is a complete thought. It has a subject and a predicate.) ➔ *Manuel joined the basketball team; remarkably, the 5′4″ young man excelled at the sport.*

✔ Between elements in a series that uses commas ➔ *The possible dates for the potluck dinner are Thursday, June 5; Saturday, June 7; or Monday, June 9.*

Colons

✔ Between two complete ideas when the second idea explains the first ➔ *Keira had a sharp, sudden memory pop into her head: the time she and her grandfather went sailing.*

✔ Before a list ➔ *Grandma brought Charlize's three favorite sweets: caramel candies, sour tarts, and bubblegum lollipops.*

✔ Between titles and subtitles ➔ *Measurement: Translating into Metric*

✔ Between volumes and page numbers ➔ *Marvel Comics 21:24*

✔ Between chapters and verses ➔ *Job 4:12*

✔ Between hours and minutes ➔ *It's 2:00 A.M.—time to sleep.*

Apostrophes

✔ Where letters or numbers have been deleted—as in a contraction ➔ *I looked at my father and whispered, "It's (It is) okay to cry every so often."*

✔ At the end of a name where there is ownership. (Remember to also add an *s* after the apostrophe if the word or name does not end in an *s* already.) ➔ *Mary Jane's horse sprained his ankle during practice.*

Commas

✔ Between items in dates and addresses ➔ *Michael arrived at Ellis Island, New York, on February 14, 1924.*

✔ Between words in a list ➔ *The university hired a woman to direct the bursar's, financial aid, and registrar's offices.*

✔ Between equally important adjectives (Be careful not to separate adjectives that describe each other!) ➔ *The reporter spoke with several intense, talented high school athletes.*

✔ After a tag that precedes a direct quote ➔ *David whined, "I am famished."*

✔ In a quote that precedes a tag and is not a question or an exclamation ➔ *"I am famished," whined David.*

  ✔ Around nonessential clauses, parenthetical phrases, and appositives (A **nonessential** or **nonrestrictive clause** is a word or group of words that are not necessary for the sentence's completion; a **parenthetical phrase** interrupts the flow of a sentence; and an **appositive** is a word or group of words that rename the noun preceding them.) ➔ *Matt's mother, Janie* (appositive)*, who has trouble with directions* (nonessential clause)*, had to ask for help.*

  ✔ After introductory words, phrases, and clauses ➔ *Hoping for the best, we checked our luggage.*

  ✔ Before conjunctions (**Conjunctions** are words that link two independent clauses together.) ➔ *Drew wanted to experience ballroom dancing before his wedding, so he signed up for lessons at a local hall.*

If you are not sure that punctuation really is *that* important, check out what happens when you move it around a little.

An English professor wrote the words "Woman without her man is a savage" on the blackboard and asked his students to punctuate it correctly.

The men wrote, "Woman, without her man, is a savage."
The women wrote, "Woman: Without her, man is a savage."

On the other hand, which "Dear Sam" letter would you want to get?

Dear Sam,
I want someone who knows what a relationship is all about. You are honorable, warm, considerate. Individuals who are unlike you concede to being incompetent and sleazy. You have destroyed me for others. I long for you. I have no emotions at all when we're separated. I can be euphoric—will you let me be yours?
Lara

Or

Dear Sam,
I want someone who knows what a relationship is. All about you are honorable, warm, considerate individuals, who are unlike you. Concede to being incompetent and sleazy. You have destroyed me. For others, I long. For you, I have no emotions at all. When we're separated, I can be euphoric. Will you let me be?
Yours,
Lara

► **Know It All!**

Can you capitalize and punctuate the following info correctly? Give it a try!

> believe it or not the great pyramid of cheops in egypt was constructed with enough stone to make a brick wall 20 inches high that could go around the world on the other hand the pentagon the largest modern building in the country would only make a brick wall two inches high that would go around the world isnt that amazing

Think you have it all? Now compare your answers with the same sentences that follow.

> Believe it or not, the Great Pyramid of Cheops in Egypt was constructed with enough stone to make a brick wall 20 inches high that could go around the world! On the other hand, the Pentagon, the largest modern building in the country, would only make a brick wall two inches high that would go around the world. Isn't that amazing?

Okay, it's time to put your capitalization and punctuation skills to the test with some practice questions.

► **Practice**

For the following questions, circle the word or words that need a capital letter.

1. My physician dr. Holly Watts told me that I was healthy enough to run the annual marathon in boston.

2. Alan Farnham, jr., was so lazy that no one in the southwest wanted to work with him.

3. Doug shouted angrily at mom, "why am I the one who always has to do the dishes?"

Choose the punctuation mark that is needed in each of the following sentences.

4. "I can't believe it!" shouted Karen. My blue socks have holes in them!"

   a. .

   b. ,

   c. !

   d. "

5. The following are my favorite foods biscuits, gravy, mashed potatoes, and French-cut green beans.

   a. :

   b. ,

   c. .

   d. ;

6. Max was so angry that he stalked out he came back 15 minutes later.

   a. ;

   b. ,

   c. ?

   d. !

7. "I wonder" Syad mused, "if he knew what he did was wrong."

   a. ?

   b. ,

   c. :

   d. ;

For each question, find the sentence that has a mistake in capitalization or punctuation.

8. a. My favorite season is Spring.

   b. Last Monday, Aunt Ruth took me shopping.

   c. We elected Ben as treasurer of the freshman class.

9. a. My best friend is moving to another city.

   b. "What time does the movie begin?" he asked.

   c. The boys' wore identical sweaters.

10. a. She asked me, to show her how to make an apple pie.

   b. He shouted from the window, but we couldn't hear him.

   c. Occasionally, someone will stop and ask for directions.

11. a. Science and math are my two best subjects.

  b. We met senator Moynihan at a conference last June.

  c. Her favorite song of all time was U2's "With or Without You."

12. a. When you come to the end of Newton Road, turn left onto Wilson Blvd.

  b. A small river runs alongside the highway.

  c. We learned that cape Cod was formed 20,000 years ago.

▶ Answers

1.   The following words should be circled: *dr., boston.*

2.   The following words should be circled: *jr., southwest.*

3.   The following words should be circled: *mom, why.*

4. d. A quotation mark (") should be placed before the word *My.*

5. a. A colon (:) should be place after the word *foods.*

6. a. A semicolon (;) should be placed after the word *out.*

7. b. A comma (,) should be placed after the word *wonder.*

8. a. *Spring* should not be capitalized.

9. c. There should not be an apostrophe after the word *boys.*

10. a. The comma is unnecessary and should be deleted.

11. b. *Senator* should be capitalized because it refers to a particular senator.

12. c. *Cape Cod* is a proper noun, and both words should be capitalized.

Sentence Structure from the Simple to the Complex

Behold the sentence. It is a major building block of everything you read today, yet often taken completely for granted. It is not just a line of words in a row; it is a line of words in a row that make *sense*! Although you can mix them up a little bit, for the most part, these words stay in a certain order so that anyone reading them can also understand them. Take a look at this sentence:

Ever best vampire hit the television Angel had to be the airwaves.

All the words are English—but you probably read it and said, "WHAT?! I don't get it. Is this a puzzle?" Yes, in a way, it is a puzzle, because things are in the wrong order. Here are the words in the right order:

The best vampire to ever hit the television airwaves had to be Angel.

▶ Feeling So Incomplete

Sentences can come in all shapes and sizes, but they have one thing in common: Every sentence must have at least a *subject* and a *predicate*. The **subject** is the focus of the sentence;

it is the *who* or the *what* the sentence is about. The **predicate** describes the subject; it explains what the subject is or what the subject is doing. The completed idea is called a **clause**, and it is the building block of all sentences.

If sentences are missing either the subject or predicate, they are an incomplete sentence, also known as a **fragment**. Here are some examples:

"Buffy the Vampire Slayer," which was on television for seven years.

Anything missing? Yes! The *predicate*. Here is another one that seems to be right—but it isn't:

On the other hand, "Angel" that made it on air for only five seasons.

Notice that both of these would be complete sentences if you took out *which* and *that*. Now let's take a look at some incomplete sentences that are missing the subject:

Going on nightly patrol, looking for vampires who automatically are experts at martial arts of all kinds.
Shifting from "Buffy" to "Angel" in a most unexpected and last-minute plot twist.

When you read these sentences, you most likely do not respond with "HEY! Where did the subject/predicate go?" Instead, you probably react with "HUH? These sentences don't make sense." You can tell *something* is missing. That response is pretty trustworthy, too. Trust your instincts when you write your own sentences. Read them over. Do they feel or sound wrong to you? It could be because something important is missing. Make sure you have both essential parts: the subject (noun) and the predicate (verb).

▶ Helpful Words to Know

Here are some other key terms to keep in mind when constructing a sentence:

Independent clause: a clause that expresses a complete thought ➔ *Tanisha walked on the grass.*

Dependent (subordinate) clause: a clause that does not express a complete thought ➔ *Although it was wet*

A complete thought ➔ *Although it was wet, Tanisha walked on the grass.*

Essential clause: a dependent clause that is necessary to the basic meaning of the completed sentence ➔ *who are pregnant* (*Women who are pregnant usually crave salty and sweet foods.*)

Nonessential clause: a dependent clause that is not necessary to the basic meaning of the completed sentence ➔ *who growls whenever the phone rings* (*Elmo, who growls whenever the phone rings, tried to attack the vacuum cleaner.*)

Phrase: a group of words that lacks either a subject or a predicate ➔ *In early spring* (*In early spring, I notice a change in people's attitudes.*)

Appositive: a phrase that makes a preceding noun or pronoun clearer or more definite by explaining or identifying it ➔ *rice pudding and fruit salad* (*Candice's grandfather brought her favorite desserts: rice pudding and fruit salad.*)

Fragment: a phrase punctuated like a sentence even though it does not express a complete thought ➔ *Timothy saw the car. And ran.*

Coordinating conjunction: a word that when preceded by a comma or a semicolon joins two independent and equal clauses ➔ *and, but, so, or, for, nor, yet* (*Winnie, you should spray those colognes away from you, or you will smell terrible.*)

Subordinating conjunction: a word that makes a clause a dependent clause ➔ *after, although, as, because, before, if, once, since, than, that, though, unless, until, when, whenever, where, wherever, while* (*After the tsunami, mourners covered those beaches nearest to the tragedy in roses.*)

Conjunctive adverb: a word that introduces a relationship between two independent clauses ➔ *accordingly, besides, consequently, furthermore, hence, however, instead, moreover, nevertheless, otherwise, then, therefore, thus* (*On Tuesdays, I play basketball; otherwise, I would go with you.*)

▶ Run On, Run On

Sometimes, a fragment isn't the problem. Some sentences just keep going and going. They either need punctuation or have the wrong punctuation. These sentences are known as **run-on** sentences. Here is an example:

Homework keeps me busy every night I don't get enough rest because I work until almost midnight and then I don't get enough sleep which means I wake up in the morning and I am so tired I can't think straight which means I don't do very well in class.

Need a breath yet? This sentence just rambles on and on. It needs to be separated into several sentences, and conjunctions are needed also. Try this solution:

Homework keeps me busy every night. I don't get enough rest because I work until almost midnight, which means I do not get enough sleep either. When I wake up in the morning, I am so tired that I can't think straight. This means I don't do very well in class either.

When you are writing your essay, you need to make sure you don't write run-on sentences. It's easy to do—you are trying hard to fill up those lines. Doing it by rambling and writing run-ons will only hurt your score.

▶ Are You My Type?

There are four primary types of sentences: simple, compound, complex, and compound-complex. The important thing for you to remember is that using a mix of these styles improves your overall writing. If all your sentences are simple ones, your response is boring to read and even worse to score.

Here are some examples to show you the differences in sentence types:

Simple: It can have more than one subject and/or verb (although the subject or verb can be compound), as well as more than one adjective and/or adverb. It has only one independent clause, however.

> I really like the show "Whose Line Is It Anyway?" (one subject, one verb)
> Ryan Styles and Wayne Brady are my two favorite improv comedians. (compound subject, one verb)
> They act, sing, and dance like total professionals. (one subject, compound verb)

Compound: This is a sentence with more than one independent clause that is joined with either a coordinating conjunction or a semicolon.

> Stephen King is a great writer, but I like Dean Koontz even better.
> I buy books faster than I can read them, so I am quickly running out of room.
> My favorite thing to buy for the house is bookshelves; I can always find room for them.

Complex: These sentences contain one independent clause and at least one dependent clause. They use subordinating conjunctions to connect them (*although*, *while*, *since*, *because*, *until*, *even though*, etc.).

> We recently moved across the country even though it was not what our families wanted.
>
> Until we moved to the Pacific Northwest, we had no idea the country was so beautiful.
>
> With mountains and coastline within two hours of driving, Oregon is a perfect place to live.

Compound-Complex: This is the biggest of the bunch. It has at least two independent clauses and at least one dependent clause. (Almost makes your brain start to fry, doesn't it?)

> When the weekend comes, we love to rent a movie and then we pop some popcorn and watch the movie together.
>
> I planned to work all weekend, but I didn't because the weather was just too nice.
>
> Why does the weekend go so fast while the week is slow and Monday is forever?

When you write your essay, there is obviously no time (and no need) for you to dwell on whether you have a compound or a complex sentence every time you write something. In fact, if you did, it would most likely be disastrous, as you would lose your focus and perhaps blow your time limit.

The key here is to familiarize yourself with these sentence types so that they become a natural part of your everyday writing. When you finish writing your response to the ACT prompt, you can use your proofreading time to make sure you used a combination of sentence types. Trust me—variety will give your response style and liveliness.

KNOW IT ALL!

Look at the following sentences. There are two fragments and two run-ons. Can you fix them? (There are different ways to fix these sentence errors.)

"World of Warcraft," which is one of the most popular online games in existence today.
Because it is a role-playing game, there is no way to actually win it, you can train and level up, however.
You can play with people all over the country there are millions of players nationwide.
Being a troll, an orc, an undead, a night elf, or a variety of other characters.

▶ Practice

Fill in the blank with the word that creates the most logical sentence. (Hint: Use a dictionary to determine which word best completes each sentence's meaning.)

1. Zuri had a bad cold. _____, he decided not to go to the movie with us.
   a. Therefore
   b. Meanwhile
   c. However
   d. Anyway

2. _____ she waited for the bus to arrive, Julia sat on the bench and read her book.
   a. So that
   b. While
   c. Even if
   d. Besides when

3. Joelle's favorite beverages are herb tea and mineral water. Chelsea, _____, drinks only milk or juice.
   a. however
   b. therefore
   c. then
   d. too

4. My dog Bumper is afraid of thunder; _____, when there's a storm I cover his ears.
   a. mainly
   b. yet
   c. moreover
   d. consequently

Choose the sentence that best combines the underlined sentences.

5. Recently, there have been government cutbacks in funds. Experts foresee steady hiring in the government's future.
   a. Despite recent government cutbacks in funds, experts foresee steady hiring in the government's future.
   b. Whereupon recent government cutbacks in funds, experts foresee steady hiring in the government's future.
   c. So that there have been recent government cutbacks in funds, experts foresee steady hiring in the government's future.
   d. Nonetheless, there have been recent government cutbacks in funds, experts foresee steady hiring in the government's future.

6. The federal government has diversity of jobs and geographic locations. The federal government offers flexibility in job opportunities that is unmatched in the private sector.
   a. In spite of its diversity of jobs and geographic locations, the federal government offers flexibility in job opportunities that is unmatched in the private sector.
   b. No matter its diversity of jobs and geographic locations, the federal government offers flexibility in job opportunities that is unmatched in the private sector.
   c. Because of its diversity of jobs and geographic locations, the federal government offers flexibility in job opportunities that is unmatched in the private sector.
   d. The federal government has diversity of jobs and geographic locations, so it offers flexibility in job opportunities that is unmatched in the private sector.

7. The Greeks thought that the halcyon, or kingfisher, nested on the sea. All birds nest on land.
   a. Whereupon all birds nest on land, the Greeks thought that the halcyon, or kingfisher, nested on the sea.
   b. The Greeks thought that the halcyon, or kingfisher, nested on the sea, but all birds nest on land.
   c. Whenever all birds nest on land, the Greeks thought that the halcyon, or kingfisher, nested on the sea.
   d. The Greeks thought that the halcyon, or kingfisher, nested on the sea, as all birds nest on land.

8. There have been great strides in the practical application of quantum physics in the last decade. We are no closer to actually understanding it than were the physicists of the 1920s.

   a. Unless there have been great strides in the practical application of quantum physics in the last few decades, we are no closer to actually understanding it than were the physicists of the 1920s.

   b. In the last few decades, we are no closer to actually understanding it than were the physicists of the 1920s, until there have been great strides in the practical application of quantum physics.

   c. Although there have been great strides in the practical application of quantum physics in the last few decades, we are no closer to actually understanding it than were the physicists of the 1920s.

   d. In the last few decades, if there have been great strides in the practical application of quantum physics, we are no closer to actually understanding it than were the physicists of the 1920s.

9. Most species of the bacterium Streptococcus are harmless. Some species of Streptococcus are dangerous pathogens.

   a. Whereas most species of the bacterium Streptococcus are harmless, some are dangerous pathogens.

   b. Because most species of the bacterium Streptococcus are harmless, some are dangerous pathogens.

   c. As most species of the bacterium Streptococcus are harmless, some are dangerous pathogens.

   d. Because most species of the bacterium Streptococcus are harmless, some are dangerous pathogens.

10. Watching a TV show is a passive behavior. Playing a computer game is an interactive one.

    a. Watching a TV show is a passive behavior, or playing a computer game is an interactive one.

    b. Watching a TV show is a passive behavior, for playing a computer game is an interactive one.

    c. Watching a TV show is a passive behavior, but playing a computer game is an interactive one.

    d. Being that playing a computer game is an interactive one, watching a TV show is a passive behavior.

11. Socrates taught that we should question everything, even the law. He was both greatly loved and profoundly hated.
   a. That he was both greatly loved and profoundly hated, Socrates taught that we should question everything, even the law.
   b. Socrates taught that we should question everything, even the law, so he was both greatly loved and profoundly hated.
   c. Socrates taught that we should question everything, even the law, which he was both greatly loved and profoundly hated.
   d. Socrates taught that we should question everything, even the law, for he was both greatly loved and profoundly hated.

12. The symptoms of diabetes often develop gradually and are hard to identify at first. Nearly half of all people with diabetes do not know they have it.
   a. The symptoms of diabetes often develop gradually and are hard to identify at first, so nearly half of all people with diabetes do not know they have it.
   b. The symptoms of diabetes often develop gradually and are hard to identify at first, yet nearly half of all people with diabetes do not know they have it.
   c. Nearly half of all people with diabetes do not know they have it, and the symptoms of diabetes often develop gradually and are hard to identify at first.
   d. The symptoms of diabetes often develop gradually for nearly half of all people with diabetes do not know they have it and are hard to identify at first.

13. I must buy some new shoes to wear to the prom. My date, Donnie, will be upset if I wear my flip-flops.
   a. Unless my date, Donnie, will be upset if I wear my flip-flops, I must buy some new shoes to wear to the prom.
   b. I must buy some new shoes to wear to the prom, and my date, Donnie, will be upset if I wear my flip-flops.
   c. I must buy some new shoes to wear to the prom, for my date, Donnie, will be upset if I wear my flip-flops.
   d. My date, Donnie, will be upset if I wear my flip-flops while I must buy some new shoes to wear to the prom.

14. I must buy my dog a new license. If I don't, I will have to pay a fine.
   a. I must buy my dog a new license, and I will have to pay a fine.
   b. I must buy my dog a new license; I will have to pay a fine.
   c. Unless I buy my dog a new license, I will have to pay a fine.
   d. I will have to pay a fine because I must buy my dog a new license.

15. <u>Art is found not only in the museum or concert hall. Art can be found in the expressive behavior of ordinary people as well.</u>

    a. Art can be found not only in the museum or concert hall, and it can be found in the expressive behavior of ordinary people, as well.

    b. In the museum or concert hall, art can be found not only there and in the expressive behavior of ordinary people, as well.

    c. Although in the expressive behavior of ordinary people, as well, art can be found not only in the museum or concert hall.

    d. Art can be found not only in the museum or concert hall, but in the expressive behavior of ordinary people as well.

▶ Answers

1. a. *Therefore* best completes the sentence's meaning; it creates a cause-and-effect relationship between Zuri's cold (the cause) and Zuri's decision not to attend the movie that night (the effect).

2. b. *While* suggests that two things are happening simultaneously; it is the only logical choice. Choice **a** implies that Julia could control when the bus would arrive. Choices **c** and **d** are unclear.

3. a. *However* indicates an impending contradiction; it is the best choice because the two clauses compare tastes. In this case, the comparison contrasts Joelle's beverage preferences to Chelsea's.

4. d. The dog's ears are covered because he is afraid of thunder; one is the effect of the other. *Consequently* means "following as an effect" or "as a result." This is the best choice.

5. a. The word *Despite* establishes a logical connection between the main and subordinate clauses. *Whereupon* and *So that* (choices **b** and **c**) make no sense. Choice **d** is both illogical and ungrammatical.

6. c. The subordinator *Because* in choice **c** establishes the logical causal relationship between the subordinate and main clauses; choices **a** and **b** do not make sense. Choice **d** has faulty construction.

7. b. *But* (in choice **b**) is the logical subordinator, establishing contrast. The others make no sense.

8. c. The subordinator *Although* shows a logical contrasting relationship between the subordinate and main clauses. The other choices do not make sense.

9. a. The subordinator *Whereas* (choice **a**) correctly establishes a contrast between the subordinate and main clauses. The other choices point to an illogical causal relationship.

10. c. The conjunction *but* sets the reader up for a contrast or opposite.

11. b. The conjunction *so* indicates a causal relationship: Socrates taught [something obviously controversial], . . . so he was . . . both loved and . . . hated. Choice **c** is incorrect because it has a misplaced modifier.

12. a. The conjunction *so* indicates that there is a causal relationship between the two main clauses.

13. c. In this sentence, the conjunction *for* means "because" and prepares the reader for a logical causal relationship.

14. c. The word *Unless* sets up the causal relationship between the two clauses in the sentence. The other choices are illogical.

15. d. The subordinator *but* contrasts the main clause and subordinate clause in a logical way. Choices **a, b,** and **c** do not make sense.

Peaceful Pronouns and Serene Subjects—Grammar in Agreement

Can't we all just get along? Have you heard someone say that about anything from classmates to the major countries in the world? Most likely, you never thought about this phrase when considering agreement between nouns and verbs. But, if your nouns and verbs don't "get along," it will hurt your essay. So, let's dive into the scintillating topics of subject-verb agreement and pronoun-antecedent agreement.

▶ Hints That Help

I'd like to give you special clues and tricks that make this not only easier, but also more enjoyable. Can you spot the error in the following conversation?

"Earl, the tires on the dune buggy needs replacing."
"Myriah, that front left wheel from the city dump are still in good shape!"

Of course, you did! The subjects and the verbs are not agreeing with each other.

What is the subject in the first sentence? *Tires.*
Is it singular or plural? Plural.
What is the verb in the first sentence? *Needs.*
Is that singular or plural? Singular.

BINGO! The first sentence should read:
"Earl, the tires on the dune buggy **need** replacing."

How about the next sentence?
What is the subject? *Wheel.*
Is it singular or plural? Singular.
What is the verb? *Are.*
Is that singular or plural? Plural.

It should read:
"Myriah, that front left wheel from the city dump **is** still in good shape!"

It is essential to remember to have your subject and verb match. If one is plural, so is the other. If one is singular, so is the other.

How about a compound subject? Again, a compound subject is when you have more than one subject connected by *and*. In this case, you also need a plural verb form. Here's an example:

Burt's uncanny ability to play the spoons and his fondness for storytelling **have** made him a huge hit at parties.

Need another one? If you insist . . .

During the game, the driver and his passengers **walk** calmly around the car.

▶ We're Not There Quite Yet

If you think you've got it, here is my chance to throw a monkey wrench into the situation. If the two subjects are about the same person or thing, treat them as singular.

Oregon's mountains and coast **makes** the state very popular with tourists.

Hold on. Not done yet. When a compound subject is preceded by *each* or *every*, treat it as singular.

Every man, woman, and child **runs** for cover when my boyfriend picks up a bowling ball.

More agreements to come! If you have compound subjects connected by *or* or *nor*, the verb should agree with the subject closest to it.

Two tubes of lipstick or a case of soda **is** the requirement to get into the party.
A case of soda or two tubes of lipstick **are** the requirements to get into the party.

Most of these are actually common sense, and if you read them aloud or even in your head, you can often tell if they are right or not. Some words, however, known as **indefinite pronouns**, drive us all a little nuts. Here is an indefinite pronoun chart for you to put up on your mirror, so you can look at it every single day. (Okay, that might be a stretch.)

ALWAYS TAKES A SINGULAR VERB	ALWAYS TAKES A PLURAL VERB	TAKES EITHER PLURAL OR SINGULAR VERBS
another	both	all
anyone	few	most
anything	many	none
each	several	some
either		
neither		
nobody		
no one or one		
someone		
something		

▶ Practice

Circle any subject-verb agreement errors in the following sentences.

1. Every decade, a few popular television shows transcends mere cleverness and high ratings to reflect the social issues of our times.

2. Here are one of the two books you left in my car yesterday afternoon.

3. The staff at the university library deserve recognition for helping locate the many sources needed for the successful completion of my doctoral dissertation.

4. During the winter season, homeowners should change their disposable furnace filters at least once a month; a dirty filter reduce furnace efficiency.

5. The chief executive officer and the chairman of the board agrees that the new benefit package should include a dental health plan as well as eye care.

▶ Answers

1. There is an error in subject-verb agreement. The subject, *television shows*, is plural and requires a plural verb form. In this case, the correct form is *transcend*, not the singular form *transcends*.

2. There is an error in agreement. The singular noun *one* requires the singular verb *is*. When the subject (in this case, *one*) follows the verb, as in a sentence beginning with *here* or *there*, be careful to determine the subject. In this sentence, the subject is not the plural noun *books*.

3. There is an error in subject-verb agreement. The singular collective noun *staff* requires a singular verb form. Therefore, the plural form *deserve* should be replaced with the singular *deserves*.

4. There is no subject-verb agreement in the first independent clause. The subject of the second independent clause is *filter*, a singular noun. Therefore, the singular form of the verb should be used. The verb *reduce* should be replaced by the verb *reduces*.

5. This sentence has a problem with subject-verb agreement. The two subjects of the sentence, *chief executive officer* and *chairman of the board*, require a plural verb. In this case, the singular form *agrees* should be replaced by the plural form *agree*.

Tense? Who's Tense? Not Me. (Or, am I?)

Y ou may think that studying and preparing for this important test is making you tense enough already, but the tense we are talking about here has nothing to do with being uptight, worried, or stressed. This tense refers to the use of verbs.

The way we know *when* something happened is through the use of tense. How the verb is spelled tells you if an event *has happened* (in the past), *is happening* (in the present), or *will happen* (in the future).

▶ The Past Tense

How does a verb change to indicate something that happened in the past? Most of the time, the suffix *-ed* is added. Simple enough, but of course, it can't stay this way. Verbs that simply need an *-ed* are called **regular verbs**. Naturally, there are **irregular verbs**. This means that to change them into the past tense, they not only get a different ending, but also often change their spelling. Give me examples, you beg. While there are many irregular verbs, here are some of the most common in the present and past tense.

IRREGULAR VERBS	
PRESENT	**PAST**
become	became
begin	began
bring	brought
do	did
eat	ate
hold	held
ride	rode
run	ran
shake	shook
shrink	shrank
speak	spoke
swim	swam
teach	taught
take	took
write	wrote

Can you think of any others?

▶ The Present and Future Tenses

To form the present tense of a verb, you often add the suffix *-ing*. To form the future, you add the word *will*. The important thing you have to remember about verb tense when you write your essay is to pick one and stick with it throughout your writing. If you are talking about the time you went fishing with your family, then keep your writing in past tense. If you are writing about how you are hoping to go to Europe some day after college, keep your writing in future tense.

Look at this example to see what I mean:

The rock legend took one more bow and then he walks off the stage. He is leaving and he met some his groupies out in the hallway. I was one of them. I smiled at him and he will smile at me, too. I think he likes me.

How do you feel after reading this? Are you confused? Did the concert just end? Is the speaker seeing the star right now or in the past? It is confusing. Let's see what happens when the verb tense is maintained throughout the example:

The rock legend took one more bow and then walked off the stage. He left and met some of his groupies out in the hallway. I was one of them. I smiled at him and he smiled at me, too. I think he liked me.

Now everything is in the past and it makes more sense. You can even make a little mantra from it: It all makes sense if you just watch tense!

When you go over your essay, check your tenses. If you shift as you write, your message will be confusing, your reader will be lost, and your ACT Writing score will go down.

▶ The Voice of Verbs

Well, you now know that verbs come in regular and irregular forms. Here is another piece of endlessly fascinating news for you: Verbs have a voice.

"Huh?" you're thinking.

"Not possible!" you exclaim. "I have never heard a verb talk to me. I think I would have noticed."

In this case, the voice is a silent one, but it is still there. This voice is known as active or passive. What is the difference? I am so glad that you asked, although if you hadn't, I would have told you anyway.

A verb is **active** when the subject performs the action. Here is an example:

I watched the man turn into a werewolf. The pixie just ignored the whole thing. (*I* am doing the action in the first sentence and the *pixie* is doing the action in the second sentence.)

A verb is **passive** when its action is performed upon the subject instead. Here is another example:

A man turned into a werewolf and was watched by me. He was ignored by the pixie.

The actions are performed upon the subjects. Notice that the passive form is wordier and more awkward. That is mainly why the active voice is almost always preferred over the passive one. When you are writing your essay, keep the verb voice in mind. Glance over your work and see if you have primarily used the active voice.

> To help illustrate the silliness of regular and irregular verbs, read the following poem. It says it all.
>
> A boy who swims may say he swum,
> But milk is skimmed and seldom skum,
> And nails you trim; they are not trum.
> When words you speak, these words are spoken,
> But a nose is tweaked and can't be twoken.
> And what you seek is seldom soken.
> If we forget, then we've forgotten,
> But things we wet are never wotten,
> And houses let cannot be lotten.
> The things one sells are always sold,
> But fog dispelled is not dispold,
> And what you smell is never smold.
> When young, a top you oft saw spun,
> But did you see a grin ever grun,
> Or a potato neatly skun?
>   —Anonymous

▶ Practice

Fill in the blank with the correct verb form.

1. On February 27, 1995, the fire department responded to a blaze that _____ at the Icarus Publishing Co. warehouse.
   a. breaks out
   b. will break out
   c. had broken out
   d. is breaking out

2. Gary Talerino and Jennifer O'Brien attended a dance that the school _____.

   a. sponsors

   b. will sponsor

   c. is sponsoring

   d. sponsored

3. I am trying to become more skilled at weaving before winter _____.

   a. arrived

   b. will have arrived

   c. will arrive

   d. arrives

4. We have _____ more of these strange pods because those people moved in next door.

   a. saw

   b. been seeing

   c. been seen

   d. see

5. The main problem Jim had _____ too many parking tickets.

   a. will have been

   b. were

   c. will have

   d. was

6. On Wednesday, Jamal and Jennifer were called to the principal's office and praised for helping a student who _____ on the icy sidewalk.

   a. falls

   b. would fall

   c. had fallen

   d. has fallen

7. The little boy _____ himself down on the floor and threw a tantrum.

   a. flings

   b. flinged

   c. flung

   d. fling

Rewrite the following passive sentences into active sentences.

8. The ACT Writing Test will be completed by me.

_____

_____

9. The storefront was being painted by Jerome when I arrived.

_____

_____

10. The vicious rumor must have been started by the rival high school's team mascot.

_____

_____

▶ Answers

1. c. The sentence requires a verb in the past tense.

2. d. The sentence requires a verb in the past tense.

3. d. The appropriate tense for this verb is the present tense.

4. b. The verbal form *been seeing* fits with the verb *have*.

5. d. The verb *was* agrees with its subject, *problem*, and is in the past tense.

6. c. Because the action takes place in the past, the only correct choice is *had fallen*.

7. c. The correct verb form is the past tense *flung*.

8. Answers will vary. One solution: I will complete the ACT Writing Test.

9. Answers will vary. One solution: Jerome was painting the storefront when I arrived.

10. Answers will vary. One solution: The rival high school's team mascot must have started the vicious rumor.

Tell Me More, Tell Me More! Modify! Metaphor!

Have you ever been reading a book and just can't picture the character or the setting in your mind? You like the story, but things are not clear enough in your head. Most likely, this is because there are not enough details for your imagination to put together an image.

When you are writing your essay, you might do the same thing. You will be writing one of your supporting points, perhaps describing an experience you had, but you may forget to include the details that your readers need to understand and relate to what you are talking about.

▶ Enriching Your Essay

The main way you can make sure you write with rich and illuminating detail is by using modifiers, as well as similes and metaphors. That said, let's look at each one.

There are a variety of ways to use modifiers. The quickest and the simplest are adverbs and adjectives. These are usually single words that tell you more about a verb (**adverb**) or a noun (**adjective**). Here are just a few examples.

What do you imagine when you read this sentence?

The spider crept across the carpet toward the young girl.

Now, let's add some adjectives and adverbs to paint a more detailed picture:

The hairy eight-legged spider crept slowly across the thick carpet toward the unsuspecting young girl.

Hairy and *eight-legged* tell you more about the spider.
Slowly tells you more about how it moved.
Thick tells you more about the carpet.
Unsuspecting tells you more about the young girl.
It is far easier to picture the whole incident now, isn't it? Let's do another one.

The clouds raced overhead as the two girls headed home.

Okay, makes sense. Not too much action though. How about this?

The menacing, black storm clouds raced overhead as the two frightened girls headed directly home.

Clearly, you know more about the situation now than you did with the first sentence. There are other ways to modify your writing besides single words. You can also use phrases. For example:

Trying not to squint, I looked all over the room for my glasses.
Keeping my eye on the snake, I tiptoed over to pick up the camera.

One thing to remember about modifiers, however, is to make sure they are next to whatever it is you are describing. If you place them somewhere else, they are referred to as **misplaced** and **dangling modifiers**. For example:

With trembling hands, the microphone shook when I picked it up.
(The microphone has trembling hands?)
Whizzing past at more than 60 miles per hour, I watched the traffic go by.
(You can really move—60 miles per hour . . . impressive!)
A piece of cheesecake was in the refrigerator that I had been saving.
(What has been saved here—the cheesecake or the refrigerator?)

TRY THIS

Look at the following words. Imagine five terms you could use to describe each one of them. Reach out—stretch. Don't stick with traditional words. The more descriptive you are, the better.

Pizza

_____

_____

_____

_____

_____

Sports car

_____

_____

_____

_____

_____

Fashion show

_____

_____

_____

_____

_____

Weather

_____

_____

_____

_____

_____

Your favorite TV show

_____

_____

_____

_____

_____

Similes and Metaphors

Another way to add detail to your writing and help make it richer is through the use of similes and metaphors. Both of them compare two unlike things, but **metaphors** simply state one thing IS another, while **similes** do the same thing using the words *like* or *as*.

> She laughed like a broken vacuum cleaner.
> Kevin was such a mule sometimes.
> Her temper is an erupting volcano.
> The train roared like a hungry tyrannosaurus rex.

See how comparing the two things helped illustrate what each one is like? This helps your writing tremendously.

I highly recommend that you use modifiers, metaphors, and similes in your writing, but please do it responsibly.

TRY THIS

Finish these sentences by creating a simile or metaphor. Be creative and see what you can come up with!

Her face was as expressive as _____.

The inside of his locker looked like _____.

Her laughter was as loud as _____.

The sun was shining as bright as _____.

His outfit was like _____.

The Vim and Vigor of Vivacious Vocabulary

I just want to take a minute to impress on you two things:

Essay readers **love** natural vocabulary usage in your essays.
Essay readers **hate** pretentious vocabulary usage in your essays.

In other words, if you can bring in strong vocabulary words to use in your essays, it will help your overall score. Readers will be impressed. However, the key here is using them both appropriately and smoothly as words you already know and are familiar with. Doing this actually says a lot about you: You are well read, you have a good deal of knowledge about language, and you even know how to spell well. If it is clear that you stuck those big words in there just to try to make yourself sound better, however, now you are being pretentious, which readers hate.

▶ Different Names for the Same Thing

To give you an example (because I know you were just waiting for one), let's look at the word *said*. People really tend to overuse this word when they write. Here are just a FEW of the alternative words you could use instead:

admitted	cried	insisted
answered	disclosed	pleaded
commented	exclaimed	remarked
confessed	explained	replied
continued	implied	responded
revealed	suggested	whispered
stated	wailed	

If vocabulary is one of your strengths, then definitely use it to your advantage when you write your response. If, on the other hand, your vocabulary is pretty limited, you are better off just writing normally than attempting to throw in big words here and there. There is too much risk that you will spell them wrong or use them inappropriately—thus annoying the readers.

TRY THIS

What follows are some pretty dull, overused words. Create at least three words that could replace them and would sound better and more detailed.

walked

_____

_____

_____

girl

_____

_____

_____

people

_____

_____

_____

things

_____

_____

_____

happy

_____

_____

_____

► Homophones and Other Commonly Confused Words

Do you know when to use *accept* instead of *except*? *Ensure* instead of *insure*? *Incredulous* instead of *incredible*? Using the right word can make the difference between confusion and clarity—and have a huge impact on your ACT prompt response.

Imagine that you are reading a story to a child and you come across the following sentence:

The night sleighed the dragon.

Chances are the child would have no trouble understanding what you read, but because you see the words on paper, you can see that something is wrong: The writer has confused two different homophones. As a result, the written sentence means something very different from what the writer intended and what the child understands. Indeed, the written version is not only incorrect, but also illogical.

A homophone is exactly what its two Greek roots suggest:

homo   *phone*

same   sound

It is a word that sounds the same as another but has a different meaning. *Night* and *knight*, for example, are homophones, as are *slay* and *sleigh*, *great* and *grate*, and *bear* and *bare*. There are dozens of homophones, many of which you already know by heart and others that you may still find confusing.

It is *very* important to know your homophones and use them correctly. Otherwise, you may confuse your readers with sentences that are at best incorrect and at worst unintelligible.

The following is a list of some of the most common homophones and other frequently confused word pairs along with a brief definition of each word.

CONFUSING WORDS	QUICK DEFINITION
accept	to recognize
except	excluding
access	means of approaching; to approach
excess	extra
adapt	to adjust
adopt	to take as one's own
affect	to influence
effect (noun)	result
effect (verb)	to bring about
all ready	totally prepared
already	by or before a specified or implied time
all ways	every method
always	forever
among	in the middle of several
between	in an interval separating (two)
assure	to make certain (assure someone)
ensure	to make certain
insure	to make certain (financial value)
beside	next to
besides	in addition to

CONFUSING WORDS	QUICK DEFINITION
bibliography	list of writings
biography	a life story
breath (noun)	respiration
breathe (verb)	to inhale and exhale
breadth	width
capital (noun)	money
capital (adjective)	most important
capitol	government building
complement	match
compliment	praise
disinterested	no strong opinion either way
uninterested	unengaged; having no interest in
emigrate	leave a country
immigrate	enter a new country
envelop	surround
envelope	paper wrapping for a letter
farther	beyond
further	additional
imply	hint, suggest
infer	assume, deduce
incredible	hard to believe; unbelievable
incredulous	skeptical; disbelieving
loose	not tight
lose	unable to find

CONFUSING WORDS	QUICK DEFINITION
may be	something may possibly be
maybe	perhaps
overdo	do too much
overdue	late
personal	individual
personnel	employees
precede	go before
proceed	continue
proceeds	profits
principal (adjective)	main
principal (noun)	person in charge
principle	standard
stationary	still, not moving
stationery	writing material
than	in contrast to
then	next in time
their	belonging to them
there	in a place
they're	they are
weather	climate
whether	if
who	substitute for he, she, or they
whom	substitute for him, her, or them
your	belonging to you
you're	you are

SHORTCUT: A STITCH IN TIME SAVES NINE

You may think that you don't have the time to come up with rhymes or other mnemonic devices to remember the meanings of these commonly confused words—you have too much studying to do. But spending the time now to create something you can easily remember can save you a great deal of time later on by drastically reducing your review time. Plus, it will also help you build a stronger and more accurate vocabulary because you will be able to accurately remember the meaning of a word.

▶ How to Study Effectively

Homophones and other frequently confused words can be particularly challenging, especially when you have a limited amount of time to prepare for an exam. Here are some specific tips and strategies to help you make the most of your study time:

- Spelling is often the key to distinguishing between commonly confused words. *Meddle*, for example, differs from *mettle* only by a *d* instead of a *t*. Use this key difference to help you remember the difference in meaning as well. For example, you might remember that *meddle* with a *d* is something you <u>d</u>on't want to do unless you want to annoy others.
- Review, review, review. Use flash cards or other study strategies to review these commonly confused words until you have them memorized. And then review them again.
- **Use** these words. If you use these words in your everyday writing and conversations, you will remember which word has which meaning. Or teach them to someone else. Teaching something to another person is one of the most effective ways to master that material.
- Remember to make the most of your learning style. Use whatever study or memorization techniques work best for you. For example, if you are a visual learner, create pictures that will help you remember word meanings. If you are an auditory learner, rhymes will be more effective.
- Pay attention to details, and use them to help you remember the words and their meanings. The more carefully you read each definition and the closer you look at the spelling of each word, the more likely you are to find a way for you to remember the differences between them. For example, *appraise* has the word *praise* in it. You can associate *praise* with a good evaluation, and *appraise* means to evaluate.

- Use your ears for the commonly confused words that aren't homophones, and use the difference in pronunciation to help you further differentiate between the words.
- Don't forget to use word parts to remember meaning. Both *prescribe* and *proscribe*, for example, have the root *scrib/script*, meaning to write. Then you can remember that *proscribe* is a (written) law that <u>pro</u>hibits something.

▶ Yo Man, Chill Out—Avoiding Slang, Idioms, and Clichés

Clearly, you want the words you write for your essay to be your own. I'm not talking about plagiarism here; I'm talking about filling up your essay with slang, idioms, and clichés. Although you can use them very sparingly to illustrate a point, you should avoid them most of the time. Some people won't understand what you mean and it will give your essay an overly casual tone that you probably don't want for the ACT Writing Test.

It is easy to forget that words you may use on a regular basis are actually slang, idioms, or clichés. To help you remember, I have created yet a few more charts that will remind you. Ain't I a peach? (Hint: That's an example.)

SLANG: words that every generation uses but older generations usually hate or misunderstand . . . or just words that usually come and go pretty quickly in usage.

SOME SLANG TERMS		
bling	yo	hottie
tight	dude	chill (out)
player	wazzup?	homie
trippin'	down	sweet
dawg	sick	wack

IDIOM: an expression whose meaning is not predictable from the usual meanings of its elements; a language, dialect, or style of speaking peculiar to a people.

THE MOST COMMON IDIOMS

He gets in my hair.	Have you lost your marbles?
This idea rings a bell.	Don't bite my head off!
I am on top of the world.	Will you please lend me a hand?
Keep your eye on the ball.	He has a trick up his sleeve.
The handwriting was on the wall.	It's as plain as the nose on your face.
You have too many irons in the fire.	This is just a drop in the bucket.
This is right up/down my alley.	That's such a pain in the neck.
I cannot see eye to eye with her.	Oh, for crying out loud.
You hit the nail on the head.	Just hold your horses!
He really blew off some steam.	Keep a stiff upper lip.
Do not blow the test.	I was walking on air.
Don't make a mountain out of a molehill.	I almost jumped out of my skin.
I don't like it, but I held my tongue.	He lost his shirt on that deal.
Are you getting cold feet already?	Do you have a skeleton in your closet?
I was feeling pretty down in the dumps.	Things were touch and go for a few days.

CLICHÉ: a trite, stereotyped expression, sentence, or phrase, usually expressing a popular or common thought or idea that has lost originality, ingenuity, and impact by long overuse.

THE MOST COMMON CLICHÉS

What goes around, comes around.	Laughter is the best medicine.
Tomorrow is another day.	Every cloud has a silver lining.
Things could be worse.	There's a light at the end of the tunnel.
It's always darkest before the dawn.	It's not the end of the world.
Good things come to those who wait.	Time will tell.
No news is good news.	When it rains, it pours.

THE MOST COMMON CLICHÉS

Don't put off until tomorrow what you can do today.	There's no place like home.
A chain is only as strong as its weakest link.	That is as easy as pie.
Absence makes the heart grow fonder.	Actions speak louder than words.
Look on the bright side.	All dressed up and nowhere to go.
Don't follow in his footsteps.	Like father, like son.
Better late than never.	Let's call it a day.
There's no time like the present.	You've got too much time on your hands.
Life is bowl of cherries.	You're not out of the woods yet.
Are you going to take the easy way out?	This is child's play.

TWO

Time for Some Essay Construction

"Me fail English? That's unpossible!"

— Ralph Wiggum, "The Simpsons"

CHAPTER

Packing the Tool Box—The Writing You Do before the Essay Begins

Can you imagine trying to cook a five-course meal without first getting some recipes and going to the grocery store? How about running a marathon without first training and stretching? Could you throw a birthday party but not buy any ice cream, cake, candles, or presents first?

Some of the most important things you do in life take preparation. Sure, you can throw a spontaneous party or decide at the last minute to join a local run, but it will not turn out the same as when you take the time to prepare.

When it comes time for you to write your ACT prompt response, you need to prepare for it as much as possible. Obviously, you cannot prepare your opinion in advance without knowing the prompt topic. What you can do, however, is be very familiar with different prewriting techniques that can guide you in writing quality essays quickly. That way, once you have your prompt and the clock is ticking, you know exactly what to do.

With only 30 minutes to write your ACT response from beginning to end, you need to use every single minute as effectively as possible.

Nokomis Public Library

▶ Managing Your Time

Although you may not have as much time as you'd like to brainstorm, organize, and revise your essay, you should still go through the basic steps of the writing process. You may need to combine steps, though. Here are the suggested amounts of time you should spend on each step in the process:

Brainstorming/Organizing: 4–5 minutes
You might be tempted to skip the brainstorming/organizing step, but don't! The few minutes you spend coming up with ideas and then arranging them in a logical order will be well worth it. If you don't have some ideas and a basic plan of organization, your essay may turn out underdeveloped and disorganized.

Writing/Revising: 15–20 minutes
You don't have time to write several drafts of your essay, so you will need to revise as you go along. If you write a sentence and then think of a better way to state the idea, simply cross out the original and write the revised version immediately following it. Concentrate on getting specific ideas down rather than trying to impress the reader with big vocabulary words. You don't have time to sit and think about a better word choice for a particular idea, and shorter, clearer sentences are better than long, complicated ones that the reader may have difficulty understanding.

Proofreading: 4–5 minutes
You will be writing quickly and may make errors that you normally would not have made. Pay particular attention to spelling, run-on sentences, and fragments.

▶ Brainstorming

The ACT essay is always a persuasive essay. The quickest way to brainstorm ideas for a persuasive essay is to create a T-chart. A T-chart presents ideas, reasons, or examples for **both** sides of the issue. Why would you want to come up with ideas for both sides when you are supposed to argue only one side of the issue? There are two reasons.

First, doing this will help you choose which side to argue for (in case you haven't already decided). Completing the T-chart may also cause you to change your decision. If you can't come up with some good reasons for the side you originally chose to argue, you may want to argue the other side. Keep in mind that the scorers do not care which side of the issue you are arguing; they care only about the strength of your argument and the quality of your writing.

Second, the T-chart is helpful because even though you are going to argue only one side of the issue, you should try to at least anticipate what the arguments for the other side may be. This is helpful later on when you present a counterargument in your essay.

Consider again the prompt about the physical education issue.

> The local high school has been under immense pressure to meet high standards as measured by standardized assessment examinations. The scores on these standardized tests have been decreasing in recent years. Some school officials have proposed eliminating physical education classes in order to allow the teachers and students to concentrate more fully on the academic subjects—particularly math and language arts. Supporters of this idea believe that physical education classes are simply a waste of time and effort and that the time and resources could be better used preparing students for standardized tests. Those against this proposal believe that physical education is just as important to students' education as any academic subject.
>
> In your essay, take a position on this issue. You may write about either one of the two points of view given, or you may present a different point of view on this topic. Use specific reasons and examples to support your position.

A T-chart for this prompt may look something like this:

Issue: *eliminating physical education classes*

For	Against
— *kids often cut or try to get out of gym*	— *physical health very important for kids*
— *don't really learn anything important*	— *What would gym teachers do?*
— *no tests for physical education skills*	— *physical education builds confidence, reduces stress*

T-CHART TIPS

1. Always restate the issue above your T-chart. This will keep your essay focused.

2. Don't worry about writing complete, grammatical sentences. This is for your eyes only.

3. Use information from the prompt as much as possible.

4. Try to come up with at least three different ideas, reasons, or examples to support each side.

5. Rely on logic and experience. Obviously, you may not be an expert on the issue being presented and you do not have the time or resources to do any research to support your argument. Therefore, you must base your argument on logic and relevant personal experience.

▶ Practice

Based on the following prompt, create a T-chart of ideas supporting both sides of the issue.

> In an effort to reduce juvenile violence and crime, many towns have chosen to enforce curfews on minors under the age of 18. These curfews make it illegal for any minor to loiter, wander, stroll, or play in public streets, highways, roads, alleys, parks, playgrounds, or other public places between the hours of 10:00 P.M. and 5:00 A.M. Supporters of the curfew believe that it will reduce community problems such as violence, graffiti, and drugs. Those who oppose curfews for minors claim these laws violate the Fourteenth Amendment rights to equal protection and due process for U.S. citizens. They also believe that such curfews stereotype minors by presupposing that citizens under the age of 18 are the only people who commit crimes.

> In your essay, take a position on this question. You may write about either one of the two points of view given, or you may present a different point of view on this topic. Use specific reasons and examples to support your position.

Issue:

For	Against
—	—
—	—
—	—

▶ Organization

For a persuasive essay, the best order of organization is emphatic—from least important or weakest argument to the most important or strongest argument. A reader usually remembers what he or she read last the most, so save your best argument for last.

After you've completed the T-chart, simply number the ideas in the order in which you will write about them. You need to do this only for the ideas on the side of the chart that you are choosing. The opposition side does not need to be numbered.

▶ Time to Write

Now we'll begin discussing the actual writing process. Here are some hints to keep in mind as you begin to draft your response to a prompt:

1. Overall, the essay shows an understanding of—and a thoughtful approach—to the prompt.
2. There is a clear thesis statement.
3. The essay is not too short. The ACT essay should be at least a five-paragraph essay, with each body paragraph running about ten sentences.
4. The body paragraphs support the thesis statement with specific examples, facts, details, or anecdotes.
5. There is a logical form of organization to the overall composition (usually emphatic order), and the ideas progress logically from one to another.
6. The composition is clear and not confusing or repetitive.

Baiting the Hook—Intriguing and Interesting Introductions

H ave you ever been watching television and a commercial comes on for the evening news? They don't say, "Tune in at 11 for the latest news, weather, and sports." That is too dull to make anyone stay up a little longer to watch. Instead, they usually say, "Will this hot weather ever end? Tune in at 11:00!" or "A chocolate truck crashed on I-84 and candy bars are everywhere! Footage at 11:00!" Why do they do this? It is because they are trying to hook you. They are reaching right through the television screen and grabbing you. They want you to say, "Wow! I need to know more about that. I just cannot miss the news tonight!"

Newspaper reporters know that very same lesson. As you glance through the paper, have you noticed that the headlines are usually quite dramatic (especially those found on the checkout stand in the grocery store, which inform you that Elvis has been sighted behind the counter of a neighborhood donut shop or that your favorite celebrities are actually aliens). Journalists realize that some people only skim the paper. To grab someone's attention, it takes an intriguing headline and first sentence or two.

Many students find it difficult to write introductions; they feel like they just can't get started. Unfortunately, during the ACT Writing Test, you don't have time to sit around thinking about a great introduction for your essay. You have to write it quickly so that you can get to the main part of your essay—the body.

The typical format of an introduction flows from general to specific. That is, it begins with a sentence or two about the general topic of the essay, then uses a sentence or two to bridge between the general topic and the writer's opinion about the topic, and finally presents the specific thesis statement. The introduction does not have to be very long—three to five sentences will work in most instances.

▶ Attention-Grabbers

Part of the function of the introduction is to spark the reader's attention, so besides following the basic format of the introduction—general to specific—you should also try to make your introduction interesting. Here are some ideas for starting your introduction in an interesting manner:

1. A definition. It's sometimes good to start with a clear definition of the topic in question. Look at the following sample prompt:

> Genetic engineering is a controversial issue. Discuss the effect genetic engineering has had on society in one of the following areas: food, human reproduction, or diseases.

The introduction for this essay might begin this way:

> *Genetic engineering refers to the manipulation of a living organism's DNA or other cellular material to achieve a desired result. Genetic engineering affects each one of us every day because whether we are aware of it or not, much of the food we eat is being affected by genetic engineering.*

You don't need to be a walking dictionary to write this type of attention-grabber. Simply define the topic as clearly as you can in your own words.

2. An interesting quotation. Make sure it's interesting and related to your topic. It doesn't necessarily have to be from a famous person. If you were writing about procrastination, you might write:

Ben Franklin said, "Never put off until tomorrow what can be done today." Procrastination is one of the biggest time-wasting activities in the corporate world.

Or

"Do it today and then put it away," my grandmother always used to say. She knew how to manage time before time management became the subject of so many best-selling books.

Once again, keep in mind that you do not have time to sit for 15 minutes wracking your brain for an interesting quote. If you cannot think of one right away, choose another method to grab your reader's attention.

3. A question. Make sure it's related to your topic, and don't overdo it by asking the reader three or four questions in a row.

Is it possible to work full time, attend night classes, and still have a social life? The answer is yes, if you know how to incorporate meeting new people and maintaining established friendships into your work and school environments.

4. A very short anecdote. A few sentences of narrative related to your topic may interest the reader.

Imagine a 12-year-old boy walking in the door of his home, dropping his books onto the kitchen table, and then lighting up a cigarette while he drinks his after-school chocolate milk. This is the face of teenage smoking, and it seems a bit silly and a bit scary all at the same time. The fact is, more teens are smoking now than ever, and worse, more teens are starting to smoke earlier than ever. We might be able to change this, though, if we raise the price of cigarettes, create ad campaigns that show how "un-cool" smoking actually is, and, most importantly, encourage parents to be more involved in the choices their children make about smoking.

▶ Avoid Restating the Prompt

A common problem students have when writing essay exams is using the prompt as their introduction. Try to avoid this. It is not only a bit dull, but also dishonest—after all, you didn't write the prompt. Here's an example of introduction you **don't** want to write:

> **Prompt:** To save money spent on lighting and security at city parks, the city council is considering a law that would not allow evening activities in the parks.

> **Draft introduction:** *To save money spent on lighting and security at city parks, the city council is considering a law that would not allow evening activities in the parks. I completely disagree with this law.*

This introduction is simply a word-for-word restatement of the assignment. It isn't properly developed, and it doesn't contain a specific thesis statement.

Instead of simply restating the prompt, use key words and ideas to write your own introduction based on the prompt:

> *After a stressful day at school, I like to take a stroll through the park. During the summer when it stays light until 8:00 P.M., I feel safe. During the winter when darkness falls around 4:00 P.M., I still feel safe because there are lights and security personnel. I realize this costs quite a bit, but some of us can't get to the park any other time. That's why the city council should continue to allow evening activities at the park. Cutting out these activities will make it difficult for many people to get exercise, enjoy evening concerts, and socialize with friends and neighbors.*

This introduction uses a very short anecdote to grab the reader's attention. Then, it bridges to a general statement of the issue and finally gives a specific thesis statement.

> ### TRY THIS
>
> Here are some truly boring introductions. How could you rewrite each one to make it more interesting?
>
> *My essay about why watching television can be educational says that it really can be.*
>
> _____
>
> _____

> *The prompt I was given is all about if school should start later. Well, isn't that obvious? Of course it should. I am going to write about how schools should not go year-round like it says in the prompt.*

> _____

> _____

▶ Creating a Thesis Statement

There are two parts to creating a strong introduction for your essay. The first one we just covered pretty thoroughly: using any one of a variety of methods to write an interesting and intriguing introduction. Now, here comes the second part, which is just as important.

The introductory paragraph of your essay is where you will state your opinion on the issue presented in the prompt. What side of an issue you choose is irrelevant. That one bears repeating. *The opinion you choose to support in your essay is irrelevant.* You will not be scored lower—or higher—for being for or against something no matter what it is. You can support the idea that candy bars should be served every day at lunch or that graffiti is today's most impressive expression of art. It truly does not matter. What counts is that you DO choose one and then clearly and logically support it.

When you state your opinion, whatever it may be, it will be part of your thesis statement. Remember that term from a few years back? Let's visit it again.

A thesis statement is the sentence that states the focus of your essay. It will guide the rest of what you write: It sets your course. For example, if the prompt asks you to recall a time when you learned something completely unexpected, your thesis statement might be something like this:

> *When I was ten years old, I found out that I was a lot braver than I realized.*

If a prompt asks you whether you think security sensors should be installed at every entrance of your school, your thesis statement might read (depending on your opinion):

> *Six months ago, I would have said that security sensors were a violation of students' rights. Last week, a student pulled a knife on me in the locker room. Although I was not injured, it was a terrifying experience that I never want to go through again. Because of it, <u>today, I strongly support the installation of sensors.</u>*

The underlined sentence is your thesis statement, which you will build off to write the rest of your essay.

The introduction is introduced. The thesis statement is stated. Ready to check out that perfect body? HEY! I mean the essay's body. Pay attention.

Creating the Perfect Body— The Middle That Has Nothing to Do with Six-Pack Abs

You are off to a great start. You read the prompt, analyzed what it was asking you to do, did your prewriting, and then wrote a Nobel Prize–worthy introduction (or just a truly decent one). Now it's time to move on to the next part of your essay: the body. Typically, the body of an essay is made up of three paragraphs.

Those three paragraphs are where you will use personal stories, quotations, experiences, thoughts, facts, and anything else that you can think of to support your opinion. You will call on that TV documentary you watched while you were baby-sitting last month. You will bring in that newspaper article your dad was droning on and on about at the kitchen table the other morning. You will add that comment you heard your teacher mention in a lecture a few weeks ago. Whatever you can call on to support your opinion is great.

▶ Strong Support

The ACT essay is a persuasive essay. Persuasive essays rely on logical reasoning and facts that support the writer's viewpoint. An underdeveloped essay may contain a lot of words, but no specific reasons that will persuade the reader to agree with the writer.

You should keep in mind that the scorers do not expect you to be an expert on the issue presented in the prompt, so instead of relying on a lot of statistics to support your argument, you're going to have to rely on common sense, specific examples from your own experience or observation, and logic.

To illustrate this, take a look at a paragraph from an essay that attempts to persuade the reader to buy a cell phone. The student is certainly not an expert on cell phones, but she uses some common knowledge and common sense to develop her argument.

The following is the student's thesis for this essay:

> Purchasing a cell phone is a smart way to save money, avoid inconvenience, and be of assistance in an emergency.

The first paragraph of the essay will deal with saving money:

> Having a cell phone can actually save you a lot of money. Of course, there is a contract you must pay for on a monthly basis, but almost all cell phone plans offer the actual phone free with the contract. In addition, many companies offer start-up and change-over deals, so if you shop around, you can get the lowest price out there for a contract. You can also save on long-distance calls if you make them on your cell phone rather than your regular phone. This is because many companies offer bonus minutes, especially on the weekends. If you use those minutes for long-distance calls, you can save hundreds of dollars a year. Now there are so many bonus-minute deals that people have started using their cell phones more than their house phones for local calls. It's simply cheaper to use the minutes allotted in their plan than to rack up charges making calls from the house phone. So if you're interested in saving money, a cell phone might help you put more money in the bank.

Although readers still may not agree with this writer, they'll probably have to admit that she makes a pretty good argument. Notice that the writer uses logical reasoning and some specific examples to support her thesis. The paragraph is well developed, interesting, and sensible.

▶ The Counterargument

If you take another look at the scoring rubric, you'll see the higher-scoring essays include counterarguments. Although this is not necessary to "pass" the ACT essay, including counterarguments (sometimes called **refutations**) will definitely put your essay in the higher-scoring zone.

A counterargument occurs in your essay when you identify an opposing argument and then logically counter or refute it. That is, you show the other side's argument to be faulty in some way.

This is where the other side of your T-chart (the one that gives reasons for the side you're NOT arguing) comes in handy. Take another look at the physical education issue prompt and the sample T-chart we created to brainstorm ideas for the essay:

> The local high school has been under immense pressure to meet high standards as measured by standardized assessment examinations. The scores on these standardized tests have been decreasing in recent years. Some school officials have proposed eliminating physical education classes in order to allow the teachers and students to concentrate more fully on the academic subjects—particularly math and language arts. Supporters of this idea believe that physical education classes are simply a waste of time and effort and that the time and resources could be better used preparing students for standardized tests. Those against this proposal believe that physical education is just as important to students' education as any academic subject.
>
> In your essay, take a position on this issue. You may write about either one of the two points of view given, or you may present a different point of view on this topic. Use specific reasons and examples to support your position.

Issue: *eliminating physical education classes*

For	Against
— *kids often cut or try to get out of gym*	— *physical health very important for kids*
— *don't really learn anything important*	— *what would gym teachers do?*
— *no tests for physical education skills*	— *physical education builds confidence, reduces stress*

Let's assume you're arguing the "For" side. Although the main focus of your body paragraphs should be to present logical arguments for the reasons on the left side of this chart, you may want to include some counterarguments for the reasons on the right side of the chart. You do not have to offer a counterargument in every body paragraph of your essay. One or two would probably be enough to show the scorers that you know how to perform this particular writing skill.

One counterargument that could easily be made deals with the idea that physical education is very important for kids. You may note that this argument appears on the "Against" side of the T-chart. Here is a counterargument for that idea:

Students have the ability to participate in physical education activities outside of the school day. Many high school students are on sports teams either in school or in the community. This proposal is not about eliminating sports teams from the schools, just physical education classes. Other students participate in physical activities such as dance or karate. Students who desire good physical health have plenty of opportunities to do this without taking up precious time in the school day.

As you can see, the counterargument also does not require expert knowledge. Personal experience is enough as long as it is presented in a logical way.

Let's look at a sample essay answering the physical education issue prompt. Because we have not yet discussed conclusions, this essay includes only the introduction and body paragraphs.

(Intro) When I was in high school, I lived for gym class. A poor academic student, I excelled in sports and found the camaraderie of teams and the locker room comforting. My gym teacher was the one who actually kept me on track academically by asking about homework and upcoming tests. Without the friendship and physical release I got from physical education, I probably would have dropped out of school. That's why the proposal to eliminate physical education classes from high school should not go into effect. Eliminating these classes would have a negative effect on students' physical, social, and academic health and have little positive effect on standardized test scores.

(Body 1) The problem of obesity has been well publicized in the past several years. This serious health issue affects many teenagers. Obesity in high school can cause many health and psychological problems. People who are obese as children and teenagers often continue to have weight problems during adulthood. Obesity in teens and adults can lead to diabetes, heart damage, and other serious diseases. The psychological impact of being teased or ostracized because of their weight can severely damage teens' confidence levels. This is why physical education classes are so important for teen health. Many teens would get little or no physical exercise on a regular basis if it weren't for their mandatory physical education classes. Aside from the physical activity, students often learn good eating and health habits from their physical education classes. This helps reduce the number of teens with weight issues. I am sure that school officials would agree that student health is more important than test scores.

(Body 2) Socially, physical education class is a great way for students to learn and practice interacting on a number of different levels. In gym class, students learn how to work as a team. They also learn the value and fun of healthy competition. These skills are imperative in the business world. Someday, these students will get jobs where they will need to work with others and compete in an aggressive yet honest and healthy way. The team sports and friendly competitions that take place in physical education class help prepare students for life. No other academic class in the student's day affords as much opportunity to work in teams to achieve a goal or to compete with others in tasks that show immediate outcomes and rewards. Physical education class also helps students learn good sportsmanship. They learn how to win humbly and lose gracefully. Again, these are valuable assets in life where things are not always fair and no one likes a boastful winner or a sore loser. <u>Although a few students find physical education class to be a bit trying because they don't feel that they are very athletic, the majority of students have positive social experiences in gym class. Most physical education teachers are much more interested in getting the students to try new things or at least put forth an honest effort rather than showcasing star athletes.</u>

(Body 3) Finally, physical education class helps students academically. It has been shown time and again that stress affects mental ability. It has also been shown that regular physical activity helps relieve stress. These assessment exams create a great deal of stress for students. The ability to attend physical education classes on a regular basis gives students much-needed downtime and allows them to reduce their stress levels by exerting themselves physically. Healthier and less-stressed students will perform better academically. Often, the students' physical education teacher, who is also sometimes their coach on a sports team, has great influence on the students' academic life. The teacher checks up on the students and encourages them to do well in their classes so they can continue playing on a team. The ideas of trying until succeeding and problem solving are reinforced in gym class, which also helps students academically. The student who just spent the last class period trying and succeeding in sinking a lay-up in basketball may apply the same principles in his math class. He will try and try, look at the problem from different angles, or ask for advice and modeling until he succeeds in solving a complex algebra problem.

As you read the sample essay, you can see how this writer used specific examples and common sense to present his arguments. The writer incorporated some counterarguments in body paragraphs 1 and 2. He also used some ideas in body paragraphs 1 and 3 that are considered common knowledge or so well known that a reader would readily accept them. Finally, you can see how the writer used the thesis statement (underlined in the introduction) to help organize the body paragraphs. He kept his arguments in the same order they appeared in the thesis statement.

Note also that the writer steered clear of making sweeping generalizations by making sure he did not use absolutes such as *all*, *every*, or *none*. It is important to avoid these types of words in a persuasive essay when you are relying on personal observation and/or common knowledge. Unless you can cite an indisputable fact that includes an absolute, such as *Every human on earth must breathe oxygen to live*, do not use it in your essay. Doing so will defeat your argument because the statement will probably not be true. *Everyone hates gym class* is simply not a fact, and including this in your essay will make the reader question your logic.

REVISING AS YOU WRITE

Most of your revising and editing will be done while you're drafting. You may write a word or sentence and then quickly realize you need to revise or correct it. The key phrase here is *quickly realize*. You don't have time to write a sentence and then spend several minutes pondering whether or not it needs revision.

Neatness counts because if the scorer cannot read your writing, he or she cannot give you credit for your ideas. As you're writing, be as neat as possible. If you need to correct or revise something, simply draw one line through it and rewrite your new version either after it or above it. Try not to write so large that you cannot fit in some corrections later on. If you can, skip lines while you're writing so you have room for revisions and corrections.

TRY THIS

Imagine you are writing an essay about why skateboards should or should not be allowed on school grounds. Write down five ideas that come to mind that you could use as supporting points.

Point 1: _____

Point 2: _____

Point 3: _____

Point 4: _____

Point 5: _____

Now, look at each one and decide which three would be the strongest. Circle them. Those are the ones you would use if you were writing your essay.

▶ Logical Transitions

One of the ways to make sure that your essay is flowing smoothly from one place to another in a clearly sequential manner is with transitions. **Transitions** are usually single words, or occasionally short phrases, that guide your reader from one point to the next. They introduce a new idea and give the reader a clue as to what that idea will be. Transitions also give the reader clues as to how the composition and paragraphs are organized.

Your ACT response must be well organized, and the ideas must lead logically one to another. The way this is done is through effective use of transitions.

Let's look at some of these transition words in the following chart. Can you imagine how they might add flow to your writing?

TYPES OF TRANSITIONS	EXAMPLES OF TRANSITIONS
Words that ADD information	*first, second, third, furthermore, and, also, another, in addition, besides, moreover*
Words that REPEAT information	*in fact, in other words, once again, to repeat, to put it another way, that is*
Words that show COMPARISON	*as if, by comparison, compared to, in comparison, in a like manner, like, likewise, similarly, also*
Words that show CONTRAST or DIFFERENCES	*although, but, however, in contrast, in spite of, nevertheless, nonetheless, rather than, though, unlike, yet*
Words that show a TIME relationship	*after so much time, after that, at first, before, beginning, ending, beyond, during, earlier, even when, eventually, ever since, finally, following, from then on, from, to, in time, last, later, meanwhile, near, far, next, now, over, soon, still, the next day, night, then until, while, someday*
Words that LIMIT or PREPARE for an upcoming example	*for example, for instance, such as, to illustrate*

TYPES OF TRANSITIONS	EXAMPLES OF TRANSITIONS
Words that show CAUSE	*because, because of, caused by*
Words that show EFFECT or RESULT	*as a result, consequently, for this/that reason, that is why, therefore, thus*
Words that show TRUTH or GRANT OPPOSING VIEWS	*certainly, conceding that, granted that, in fact, naturally, no doubt, of course, surely, undoubtedly, without a doubt*

Jumping to Conclusions—Time to Sign Off

ook! Look again! Can you see it? Do you see that faint light flickering somewhere ahead of you? It's not Tinkerbell. It's not your imagination. It's not the light people say they see right before they die and then come back to write a book about it. Instead, it's that proverbial light at the end of the tunnel. You have read the prompt, done the prewriting, come up with a thesis, written the introduction, and supported it with great details in the body of your response. Now it's time for you to say good-bye with your conclusion. You're almost there!

The conclusion's purpose in life is to sum up what you have said. Like everything else, you can do this poorly or well.

People tend to have as much trouble writing conclusions as they do writing introductions. On the ACT, you must remember the time constraint. You should spend only a minute or so on the conclusion. The conclusion is not the place to introduce any new ideas or topics. If you have any left over, just let them go or find a place for them in the body of the essay.

The main rule to keep in mind when writing your conclusion is like the one I harped on when I was telling you about writing the introduction: Don't turn it into an announcement. The guaranteed low score conclusions start out with:

"And so, in conclusion . . ."
"To sum it all up . . ."
"I shall now conclude . . ."
"In closing . . ."

Please don't do this. The reader KNOWS it's your conclusion because it's at the bottom of the page where it is supposed to go. Instead, a strong conclusion should refer back to the original thesis statement. You want to tie your essay together by referring back to your original viewpoint expressed in the introduction. But please do not give a word-for-word repeat of your thesis statement. If your original thesis statement was "I think that curfews are too invasive to be a part of our community," then please *do not* write an concluding statement that reads, "And so, in conclusion, that is the reason that I think that curfews are too invasive to be a part of our community."

TRY THIS

Imagine you have written an essay in which your thesis statement was "I think that having an active and well-developed sense of humor is one of the most important survival techniques in the world." You have given your three examples of why you feel this way and now it is time to write your conclusion. How can you tie back to it without repeating it?

_____

_____

_____

_____

_____

_____

▶ How to End Your Essay

After writing the body of your response, it may feel like you have said everything you had to say—but you haven't. Your essay will lack a feeling of closure if you write your third supporting point and then put down your pencil. This is your chance to leave an impression on your reader, to stress the importance of your thesis statement and to bring your essay to a close.

Anecdotes

Tell an anecdote. Remember, however, that an anecdote is a very short story—an incident—that can be told in a few sentences. This is sometimes an effective way to end an essay. Again, make sure the story is related to the topic of the essay and makes some kind of point to the reader about the topic.

> **Example:** *Nursing requires the ability to work long hours without taking your exhaustion out on innocent patients. <u>I once knew a nurse who had worked 12-hour shifts at a hospital for many years. When I asked her how she obtained the energy for her job, she replied that nursing was a life choice, not simply a career choice, and that she gained her enthusiasm and stamina from the knowledge that every day she touched a life and made it better.</u>*

Solutions

You can also suggest a course of action—a solution to a problem or answers to a question. This type of conclusion works well for persuasive essays. Make sure the solution or recommendation is reasonable. It may include something the reader can do to solve a problem or something a third party—such as the government or other authorities—can do.

> **Example:** *Using natural, nontoxic cleansers in the home can reduce incidences of accidental poisoning, allergic reactions, and resistant bacterial strains. <u>Perhaps the government should make a concerted effort to inform consumers of the merits of using natural cleaners in the home as opposed to commercially made cleaning products, which often contain highly toxic substances.</u>*

Predictions

Make a prediction. Look to the future. This can take the form of something you know will happen, believe will happen, or hope will happen based on your topic and what you've written in the composition.

> **Example:** *It is time to seriously think about how we can solve the problems caused by teen vandals. There are solutions to this problem that will help keep our community free of vandalism but still allow law-abiding teenagers to enjoy their personal freedoms. <u>Hopefully, some of these solutions can be put into place soon</u>, so that our community can be beautiful and teenagers can live their lives without unnecessary restrictions.*

The Final Touches—Don't Turn It in Yet!

O h, yes. That little light at the end of the tunnel has become a spotlight now. It's so bright, you can barely stand it. The end is near—the end of the ACT Writing Test, that is. You have performed admirably—every step you needed to complete is done. Your essay is written. The last word is on paper.

Although I know you'd really like to stand up and cheer, grab your keys, and head out to spend the rest of the day thinking about anything in the world other than this essay test, there is one more thing you must do. Before you turn your precious work over to the hands of others, take a moment to go over it one more time. It is like putting wax on your car. You already washed, scrubbed, and dried it. It looks good. So just add the very last touch and add some wax—or, in this case, some proofing. It helps them both shine.

If you have plotted the rest of your time well, you should have at least five minutes to edit and proof your essay. Here are the do's and don'ts of doing so quickly and efficiently.

DO	DO NOT
Do read your essay out loud in your head and listen for any mistakes; consider reading it backward to spot errors more easily.	Do not scribble out things you want to change or edit.
Do draw a light line through the words you want to cut out.	Do not have arrows going all over the place.
Do check for errors in spelling, punctuation, and capitalization.	Do not worry about the word count or giving your essay a title.
Do check for agreement, tense, and legible handwriting.	Do not try to fill in the remaining few lines at the last minute.
Do make sure you have a clear thesis statement and supporting points.	Do not attempt any kind of major revision at this point.

In Paragraphs

You should always check for the following:

1. details, examples, and supporting evidence in each paragraph
2. incomplete thoughts
3. rambling, off-topic thoughts
4. paragraph breaks that help the reader see your main points
5. effective transitions between ideas

In Words and Sentences

Make sure your essay contains the following:

1. complete sentences (no fragments or run-ons)
2. variety in sentence structure
3. agreement
4. concise word choices
5. clichés, pretentious language, slang, or idioms
6. ambiguity
7. passive voice
8. proper punctuation and capitalization
9. correct spelling

Once you have done these things, you are ready to turn your response over to the ACT readers.

THREE

Put Your Skills to the Test— Practice Prompts and Sample Essays

"Writing is easy: All you do is sit staring at a blank sheet of paper until drops of blood form on your forehead."

— Gene Fowler

In this section, as promised, you will find 40 prompts similar to the one that you will encounter on the official ACT Writing Test. As you read the prompts, take the time to think about what position you would take on each one. Have a piece of scrap paper with you as you read and practice jotting down some of the different points you might use to support your point of view. Using your ideas, you should write sample responses. Set a timer for 30 minutes as you answer each prompt. If you are willing to practice your writing skills, you have already taken an important step toward improving your writing.

▶ Scoring Your Essay—Effectively

After you finish a response to a practice prompt, learn how to score your essay. For your reference, you can refer to the rubric on page xii of this book. To determine your score, simply refer to the categories on the rubric to see how your writing measures up. If you have difficulty figuring out your score, ask someone knowledgeable, such as a teacher, counselor, writing coach, or college professor, to help you. If this is not an option, you can refer to the four bolded writing prompts in this section. These highlighted prompts have model responses at the end of this section. The samples include top, middle-of-the-road, and low responses. In fact, you will see models at each ACT score level: 6, 5, 4, 3, 2, and 1. You can use these as benchmarks to compare and contrast your writing.

Each model response at every scoring level will be accompanied by a critique. The critique will help you see the strengths and weaknesses of the response. You will be able to understand what the ACT writing scorers are looking for—both pitfalls to avoid in your own response and the signs of "good" writing.

On to the important stuff—sharpen your pencils, get in the ACT frame of mind, and let's write! Remember to:

- Address the specific topic and writing task.
- Create a well-organized response.
- Include developed supporting ideas and specific details.
- Use sentence variety and strong word choices.

▶ Sample Prompts

1. The administrators of your school have decided that learning a foreign language should be mandatory for juniors and seniors. They are revamping the available options, however, and changing the curriculum from the traditional French, German, and Spanish to Spanish, Japanese, and Russian. In the opinion of the school, these are the three languages that will be utilized most in the future. In your view, what languages should the school teach and should they be mandatory or optional?

In your essay, take a position on this question. You may write about either of the two points of view given, or you may present a different point of view on the topic. Use specific reasons and examples to support your position.

2. Your school has decided to alter its emphasis in history classes. Instead of spending time on a variety of eras throughout time, beginning with ancient periods, the department has decided to focus on teaching history only from 1940 to the present. Proponents of this theory believe that students can learn best from studying the recent past up to the present. A few history teachers, on the other hand, believe strongly that this is an error. They advocate the idea that the only way we can understand and prepare for the future is to study as much of the past as possible. In your view, how much of history should be taught in schools?

In your essay, take a position on this question. You may write about either of the two points of view given, or you may present a different point of view on the topic. Use specific reasons and examples to support your position.

3. There is a petition circling around your school proposing a change from the traditional grading system of A, B, C, D, and F to a simple pass/fail system. There are vocal advocates on both sides. Next week, there is going to be a parent/teacher/student meeting about it, and students have been encouraged to attend so that their opinions on the matter can be heard. In your view, which system would work best for everyone involved?

In your essay, take a position on this question. You may write about either of the two points of view given, or you may present a different point of view on the topic. Use specific reasons and examples to support your position.

4. Recently, you overheard your friends talking about their part-time jobs. You had to admit that you envied them. If you had a job, you would have more spending money, learn some job skills, and perhaps gain some independence. Your parents, however, disagree. They believe that a part-time job will only excessively tire you and interfere with your ability to keep up with your classes and homework. In your point of view, should high school students have part-time jobs or should their energies be focused primarily on school?

In your essay, take a position on this question. You may write about either of the two points of view given, or you may present a different point of view on the topic. Use specific reasons and examples to support your position.

5. In an effort to reduce juvenile violence and crime, many towns have chosen to enforce curfews on minors under the age of 18. These curfews make it illegal for any minor to loiter, wander, stroll, or play in public streets, highways, roads, alleys, parks, playgrounds, or other public places between the hours of 10:00 P.M. and 5:00 A.M. Supporters of the curfew believe that it will reduce community problems such as violence, graffiti, and drugs. Those who oppose curfews for minors claim these laws violate the Fourteenth Amendment rights to equal protection and due process for U.S. citizens. They also believe that such curfews stereotype minors by presupposing that citizens under the age of 18 are the only people who commit crimes.

In your essay, take a position on this question. You may write about either of the two points of view given, or you may present a different point of view on the topic. Use specific reasons and examples to support your position.

6. Some theorists propose that the reason teenagers act, dress, speak, and behave the way they do is to differentiate them from the rest of society. According to this ideology, teens are trying to establish their individual identities by creating a persona that is as unlike other age groups as possible. Other theorists disagree; they say that this type of teenage behavior stems from an inner drive to belong or conform. They state that although teenagers do make a concentrated effort to appear "different," they all do it in the same ways, thus losing the concept of individuality. In your point of view, is teen behavior driven by a desire to stand out and be unique or to conform and blend in?

In your essay, take a position on this question. You may write about either of the two points of view given, or you may present a different point of view on the topic. Use specific reasons and examples to support your position.

7. One of the growing trends in alternative education today is home education. With a national growth rate of 15% to 20%, homeschooling has merged from a temporary fad to a viable educational option. Those in favor of homeschooling often state that it gives their children a more personal, focused, and hands-on education. Those who oppose it say that homeschooling limits both children's social and educational opportunities. In your point of view, is homeschooling something that enhances or inhibits a student's education?

In your essay, take a position on this question. You may write about either of the two points of view given, or you may present a different point of view on the topic. Use specific reasons and examples to support your position.

8. Recently, one of the philanthropic organizations your teacher is a member of has decided to create several student scholarships. The organization is trying to decide if the scholarships should be given to students based on their athletic ability, financial status, grade point average, or community involvement. Your teacher has been put in charge of gathering various opinions from the community and in doing so he has turned to you for your thoughts on the matter. In your point of view, what qualities should educational scholarships be based on?

In your essay, take a position on this question. You may write about either of the two points of view given, or you may present a different point of view on the topic. Use specific reasons and examples to support your position.

9. Some educational experts believe that schools, as a whole, spend too much time teaching isolated facts and statistics and not enough time focusing on classes that would teach common sense and necessary life knowledge. They propose that schools significantly alter their curriculum in order to implement classes in such subjects as job interview skills, budgeting, and living on your own. In your point of view, do schools focus on the wrong knowledge? What should be the school's main focus?

In your essay, take a position on this question. You may write about either of the two points of view given, or you may present a different point of view on the topic. Use specific reasons and examples to support your position.

10. In the local newspaper, you read a story about a young student at a nearby high school who had been hauled out of the classroom in handcuffs for bringing a weapon to school. She had spent the weekend helping her older brother move and in the back seat of her car was a box knife. A student had seen it there and turned her in. Because this school has a zero tolerance policy on weapons in school, she was suspended in accordance with the rules. In your point of view, how far should zero tolerance policies go in schools? Should exceptions be made or should any student possessing weapons of any kind be disciplined?

In your essay, take a position on this question. You may write about either of the two points of view given, or you may present a different point of view on the topic. Use specific reasons and examples to support your position.

11. The law regarding driving ages in your state is under review. Because of the nationwide high incidence of traffic accidents among people under the age of 21 and those over the age of 65, there is a proposal of raising the minimum driving age and establishing a maximum age. In your point of view, should driving ages be changed for both age groups or are there other alternatives that would be more effective?

In your essay, take a position on this question. You may write about either of the two points of view given, or you may present a different point of view on the topic. Use specific reasons and examples to support your position.

12. Because of the recent increase in incidents of school violence, a number of schools around the country are limiting the number of times a student can go to his or her locker. While advocates believe that this will help reduce the risk of students keeping any illegal substances (including weapons) in their lockers, others disagree. They state that it has little effect on violence and other issues, but it does drastically increase the number of books the average student has to carry around every day. In your point of view, should locker visits be limited or not?

In your essay, take a position on this question. You may write about either of the two points of view given, or you may present a different point of view on the topic. Use specific reasons and examples to support your position.

13. Your English teacher has assigned a research paper, and one of the requirements is that no more than half of your resources come from the Internet. The rest have to be from books, magazines, interviews, or personal experience. Some students are upset because they think they should be able to use the Internet for all of their resources. They argue that online sources are much more up-to-date and accessible than printed material. In your opinion, who do you think is correct? Should the teacher allow all the resources to come from the Internet like the students want or should there be a mix of materials?

In your essay, take a position on this question. You may write about either of the two points of view given, or you may present a different point of view on the topic. Use specific reasons and examples to support your position.

14. Gasoline prices have soared in recent years, hitting levels that have frequently made filling a gas tank prohibitive. Many politicians and others are working hard to lower these prices and keep them down so that the economy is not severely damaged. Other experts, however, are pleased to see this happening because they hope it forces the country to explore alternative fuel options. In your view, are continually rising gas prices going to hurt or help our world in the long run?

In your essay, take a position on this question. You may write about either of the two points of view given, or you may present a different point of view on the topic. Use specific reasons and examples to support your position.

15. A student activist group on your school campus is protesting the use of animals for dissection in science classes. The group claims that animals have the basic rights of life and happiness and that purposely destroying them for use in classes is cruel. Many of the science students disagree, stating that animals are useful in educating people about important medical and health issues and that eliminating their use in the classes would severely harm students' education.

In your essay, take a position on this question. You may write about either of the two points of view given, or you may present a different point of view on the topic. Use specific reasons and examples to support your position.

16. Many experts predict that our society will eventually become paperless. As e-mails have slowly come to replace snail mail, so do experts think that online novels will replace hand-held ones. Eventually, these experts say, libraries as we know them today will disappear. In your viewpoint, will the world depend more and more on computer resources and is this progress?

In your essay, take a position on this question. You may write about either of the two points of view given, or you may present a different point of view on the topic. Use specific reasons and examples to support your position.

17. Many people believe that the Internet has brought people closer together and made the world a much smaller place. With just the touch of a few keys, people can communicate with others on the opposite side of the planet. Some people disagree, however. They believe that the Internet has pushed us further apart. Families spend time in separate rooms talking to people thousands of miles away while they ignore the people in the next room. In your point of view, do you think that the Internet has brought us all closer or driven us apart?

In your essay, take a position on this question. You may write about either of the two points of view given, or you may present a different point of view on the topic. Use specific reasons and examples to support your position.

18. Sports have been an integral part of public schools for decades. In recent years, however, there has been a growing concern that instead of teaching cooperation, sports focus far too much on competition. Instead of learning about teamwork and the importance of working together for a common goal, some worry that school sports are actually teaching kids that winning is everything. In your point of view, do school sports teach cooperation or competition?

In your essay, take a position on this question. You may write about either of the two points of view given, or you may present a different point of view on the topic. Use specific reasons and examples to support your position.

19. Numerous studies have been done on the effects of playing violent video games on children. While some results state that these games encourage children to behave violently in real life, others seem to indicate that by taking out their violent feelings on virtual characters, kids are calmer and more tolerant to real people. In your point of view, do violent video games help kids deal with negative feelings or increase their violent tendencies?

In your essay, take a position on this question. You may write about either of the two points of view given, or you may present a different point of view on the topic. Use specific reasons and examples to support your position.

20. For several years now, a few senators have proposed a bill in Congress to abolish the production of the penny. Their statistics state that the penny almost costs more to make than it is worth. If this bill is passed, it would change our pricing systems, as nothing could be priced in increments of less than $0.05 anymore. In your opinion, do you think eliminating the penny is a wise decision or should things stay the way they are?

In your essay, take a position on this question. You may write about either of the two points of view given, or you may present a different point of view on the topic. Use specific reasons and examples to support your position.

21. In some cities in this country, certain people who have committed minor crimes or are first-time felons are allowed to do "weekend time," which means they go to jail from Friday night until Sunday morning to serve their sentences. During the week, they are allowed to go to work or attend school. Some people think this is ridiculous and that anyone who breaks the law and is sentenced to jail time should be treated more strictly. Others see this as advancement in criminal justice, helping people maintain their lives and still "pay their debt to society." In your viewpoint, are these felons being treated fairly or too leniently?

In your essay, take a position on this question. You may write about either of the two points of view given, or you may present a different point of view on the topic. Use specific reasons and examples to support your position.

22. There are a number of students in your school who are planning to graduate and head directly to some of the biggest colleges in the country. These colleges have huge campuses and thousands of students enrolled. A number of smaller colleges have been sending you promotional literature, several of which really appeal to you. In your viewpoint, do you think small or large colleges offer a better education? What factors should help a student choose a college?

In your essay, take a position on this question. You may write about either of the two points of view given, or you may present a different point of view on the topic. Use specific reasons and examples to support your position.

23. In a recent interview, a local educator said that no young person today can possibly be successful without going to college. The educator proceeded to outline the importance of a college degree to earning higher annual incomes. In your point of view, do you think this was an honest assessment of the situation? Is college an integral element of success? Why or why not?

In your essay, take a position on this question. You may write about either of the two points of view given, or you may present a different point of view on the topic. Use specific reasons and examples to support your position.

24. For the last decade, there has been a continuing push for "politically correct" language so as not to offend or upset any particular race, age group, or gender. Firemen became firefighters; policemen became police officers. This trend has made its way into many different areas of life, including education. Even textbooks have been altered in an attempt to be politically correct. In your point of view, do you think that being politically correct in your speech and writing is an acknowledgement of sensitivity to diversity or is it just pretentious and unnecessary?

In your essay, take a position on this question. You may write about either of the two points of view given, or you may present a different point of view on the topic. Use specific reasons and examples to support your position.

25. Parents and school board members have become increasingly concerned about the use of the Internet in school. Many people report that students have either purposely visited or inadvertently been exposed to websites that display text and images that are inappropriate for teenagers. These people want to set up a school Intranet that would allow access to only a few preapproved websites. Opponents of this idea state that this is censorship and does not give students enough access to valuable information on the Internet. In your opinion, should the school create an Intranet that would limit the websites students could visit or do you think this is censorship that would deny students access to valuable information?

In your essay, take a position on this question. You may write about either of the two points of view given, or you may present a different point of view on the topic. Use specific reasons and examples to support your position.

26. Numerous scientific studies have shown that teenagers have a different internal clock than young children or adults. Because of these differences, they naturally sleep in later and stay up later. In response to this new information, some junior high and high school systems have considered changing the time that schools start in the morning. They believe that by starting later, students will be more alert and learning will be easier and quicker. Those who oppose the idea believe it will result in getting out too late in the afternoon and causing problems with job schedules. In your point of view, do you think that school schedules should be altered or kept as they are?

In your essay, take a position on this question. You may write about either of the two points of view given, or you may present a different point of view on the topic. Use specific reasons and examples to support your position.

27. Cheating is on the increase nationally. In fact, more than 80% of teenagers admit to cheating at one time or another. Examples include the student who writes key information on his or her palm or who uses his or her cell phone to receive a text message with the right answers. Teachers have three challenges facing them when it comes to cheating: how to prevent it, how to catch it, and how to punish it. None of these have easy answers. In your point of view, how do you think cheating should be handled in your school? Should it be punished and if so, how? Should it be ignored? If so, what are the ramifications of that?

In your essay, take a position on this question. You may write about either of the two points of view given, or you may present a different point of view on the topic. Use specific reasons and examples to support your position.

28. Demographically, high school students make up one of the largest job-seeking groups in the country. As employers interview these young people for any variety of part-time jobs, they are often put off by the way a student dresses or colors his or her hair. They may also be bothered by tattoos and/or body piercings. For employers, this appearance does not fit what they want for their business. To these teens, they are being discriminated against for how they choose to live. In your viewpoint, which of these two groups is right? Should employers be able to make these kinds of choices or not?

In your essay, take a position on this question. You may write about either of the two points of view given, or you may present a different point of view on the topic. Use specific reasons and examples to support your position.

29. In 1969, an important case went before the Supreme Court. The question being discussed was whether or not students who were against the Vietnam War had the right to wear black arm bands to school to demonstrate their protest. In this case, the judge ruled that it should be allowed. He stated that a student's right to express him- or herself should not end when entering school grounds. Almost 40 years later, that all changed. Another case in the Supreme Court decided that a student's right to expression could not be applied to school newspapers. This time, the court said that principals had the right to edit what is printed in school newspapers. If they felt the subject matter, attitude, or opinion was not proper for students, it would not be printed. In your opinion, do you think censorship like this should be allowed within the school system or not? Was the Supreme Court right the first time or the second?

In your essay, take a position on this question. You may write about either of the two points of view given, or you may present a different point of view on the topic. Use specific reasons and examples to support your position.

30. Our society is becoming increasingly dependent on computers. Most people cannot imagine going 24 hours without using a computer in some form. Other people long for the time when society was less reliant on machines. In your opinion, have computers become such a blessing to society that to lose a connection is a real loss or are they are a detriment to society in some way?

In your essay, take a position on this question. You may write about either of the two points of view given, or you may present a different point of view on the topic. Use specific reasons and examples to support your position.

31. Last month, your school principal announced that seniors who had completed the required number of credit hours and maintained at least a B average were going to be offered two choices. They could graduate mid-year or they could be given early release each school day for the rest of the school year. You are going to vote on which option is best in your opinion. Do you think graduating months early would be the best method for students or do you think that getting out of school a few hours early each day would be preferable?

In your essay, take a position on this question. You may write about either of the two points of view given, or you may present a different point of view on the topic. Use specific reasons and examples to support your position.

32. Author Alfie Kohn believes that children are "punished with rewards," as he puts it. He believes that when children are constantly given some kind of reward for a job well done, whether good grades, gold stars, or prolific praise, they begin working hard in order to get the rewards. When rewards stop, they stop working. Children don't develop the internal pride and satisfaction from accomplishing something worthwhile. In turn, Kohn believes that this leads to unhappiness because students are externally motivated by the rewards rather than internally motivated by their goals and success. Do you think that rewards and praise help a child keep doing better and build pride or do you think that overall, rewards shift the focus from accomplishing a goal to getting a "treat"?

In your essay, take a position on this question. You may write about either of the two points of view given, or you may present a different point of view on the topic. Use specific reasons and examples to support your position.

33. Your school is attempting to organize an official policy on cell-phone use in school. School officials have finally decided that cell phones can be used on the property, but only during set hours and never in the classroom. A friend of yours has started a petition saying that it is interfering with a student's freedom of speech not to be able to use his or her cell phone during class. Do you think he is being ridiculous or does he have an important point?

In your essay, take a position on this question. You may write about either of the two points of view given, or you may present a different point of view on the topic. Use specific reasons and examples to support your position.

34. According to an article you read in a music magazine, the government is seriously considering instigating some kind of rating system for every CD produced in the country. Like movies, music would be rated as to its appropriateness for various age groups. A sticker would be added to the packaging to make this rating clear. In your viewpoint, do you think a rating system like this would make it easier to choose music that you like as well as protect younger listeners from inappropriate music or do you think this government idea is a mistake?

In your essay, take a position on this question. You may write about either of the two points of view given, or you may present a different point of view on the topic. Use specific reasons and examples to support your position.

35. In an effort to combat obesity and increase healthfulness among students, the school board is considering changing the cafeteria menu to avoid all junk food and provide only low-fat meals and snacks. They are also considering eliminating the soda machines. Supporters say this plan will help students slim down and have more energy for school. Opponents say this plan is unfair to students who will now have no choices in the cafeteria and will cost the school a great deal of money because the soda machines generate money for the school. In your opinion, do you think the schools should offer only low-fat meals and snacks?

In your essay, take a position on this question. You may write about either of the two points of view given, or you may present a different point of view on the topic. Use specific reasons and examples to support your position.

36. Recently, you heard some of your classmates talking about going to colleges outside of the United States. They were talking about the incredible opportunities they could find in other countries and how they could combine travel and education at the same time. This made you curious. Is going overseas for your college education an intriguing idea or is it better to stay in the United States where you are familiar with the culture, language, and lifestyles?

In your essay, take a position on this question. You may write about either of the two points of view given, or you may present a different point of view on the topic. Use specific reasons and examples to support your position.

37. Some people believe that school is meant to train a person for getting a job and earning a living. Others believe that the main purpose of school is to introduce students to new ideas and ways of thinking. In your viewpoint, do you think school is training ground for future employment or a way of introducing the concepts of the world to students?

In your essay, take a position on this question. You may write about either of the two points of view given, or you may present a different point of view on the topic. Use specific reasons and examples to support your position.

38. Your school library has refused to purchase any manga or graphic novels to put on its shelves. Your English teacher disagrees with this decision. She thinks that anything that encourages a student to read should be included in the library. She is organizing a meeting of students to discuss this and has invited you. In your opinion, do you think the library officials are right in choosing not to add this kind of material to their collection? Or is your English teacher right that including manga and graphic novels is a good way to persuade students to read more often?

In your essay, take a position on this question. You may write about either of the two points of view given, or you may present a different point of view on the topic. Use specific reasons and examples to support your position.

39. There is a hot debate raging in your school administration right now over whether students should be allowed access to coffee in the school cafeteria. Some of the staff strongly believe that drinking coffee is bad for young people and should be banned from the building altogether. Others feel that it is an example of age discrimination to allow the staff free access to coffee but not the students. In your viewpoint, do you think high school students should be able to drink coffee during lunch if they want to?

In your essay, take a position on this question. You may write about either of the two points of view given, or you may present a different point of view on the topic. Use specific reasons and examples to support your position.

40. Some schools are battling with the idea of whether or not to teach sex education in classrooms or not. Many feel that it is an essential component to any young person's education and that, if done properly, it can help reduce teen pregnancy and the spread of sexually transmitted diseases. Others, however, feel just as strongly that sex education belongs only in the home and that the school is stepping beyond its bounds by offering the class to students. In your viewpoint, is the proper place for sex education at home or in school?

In your essay, take a position on this question. You may write about either of the two points of view given, or you may present a different point of view on the topic. Use specific reasons and examples to support your position.

▶ Sample Answers to Prompt #5

Model Score 6

Imagine your parents or grandparents as teenagers: Do you think they were running around vandalizing movie theaters and ripping off ice cream parlors? Decades ago, our parents and grandparents enjoyed parties and late-night diner runs as much as we do today. They were not out to scandalize their communities; they simply wanted to enjoy life. Yet now, these same freedom-loving people want to suppress our freedom by enforcing a law that would prevent any teen from attending parties or working late to earn a little extra money. A curfew for minors under the age of 18 will not only have little effect on crime rates, but it will also wrongly restrict the social life and employability of many teens.

According to supporters of this legislation, enforcing a curfew on children under the age of 18 would "reduce community problems such as violence, graffiti, and drugs." There are many problems with this statement. For instance, violence does not take place in a community only at night. The events at Columbine proved that violence can take place in broad daylight, and that the root of this violence can sometimes begin at home. While graffiti is ugly and destructive, it is not only done in "alleys, parks, or playgrounds." There are scribblings and drawings on many of the desks and textbooks in my school, yet they were done in the daylight and are just as destructive. Similarly, drugs are a problem in every community and do not discriminate against any type of student or time of day. It is unfortunate but true that a student can sell drugs just as easily in school as he or she can in a park at midnight. What this law is doing is not eliminating these problems, but simply shifting them to different public places during different times of the day.

One argument of those opposed to this legislation is that "curfews stereotype minors by presupposing that citizens under the age of 18 are the only people who commit crimes." This is true. While many community problems can be attributed to minors, the same problems can also be attributed to adults. This fact is supported by the large numbers of men and women over the age of 18 in our prison system. The community may save money by keeping a few young vandals or drug dealers out of juvenile prison, but they will certainly continue to pay for those mature men and women who have chosen to support themselves by selling drugs to minors in the first place! It should also be noted that while a curfew may keep minors under the age of 18 from loitering and causing destruction, there is a group of young adults between the ages of 18 and 21 that cannot legally drink alcohol but still do. The curfew will do nothing to stop the destruction of property or even lives that may result from this action.

A curfew like this would only restrict the positive outlets many teenagers have, such as healthy interaction with their peers and work. Many teens have long days filled with school and after-school activities such as sports or clubs, chores, and homework. Most of my friends do not even have a free moment until about 9:00 or 10:00 p.m. It is then that many teens go out and see a movie or visit with friends. This curfew would all but prevent most teens from being able to socialize with other teens in person. Teenagers would be relegated to online and phone friendships. Another problem with this curfew is that it would prevent many teens from having a job, which many teens need. Many jobs for teenagers are at fast-food restaurants where the late-night shifts are the only ones teens are able to get because they are in school all day long. This curfew would make it very difficult for teens to obtain jobs and earn money for college. Social interaction and work are both healthy experiences that make teens into good, productive community members. This curfew would prevent that.

Obviously, by encouraging this legislation, the supporters of this curfew feel they are protecting their rights as well as those of the community. The minors of previous generations have grown up to be mature and responsible citizens with legitimate concerns about youth and community. While there may be more evils lurking in society than in decades past, these people must realize that putting a time limit on problems cannot solve them. Perhaps instead of trying to contain them, their time would be better spent finding the root of the crime, violence, and drug problems that are rampant in our society today. By working these troubles out instead of locking them in, it is possible that both adults and minors may work together to make our community a better place.

Critique

This essay shows an excellent and insightful understanding of the prompt. It clearly addresses the prompt. The student creates a clear and creative opening and closing, and the point of the essay is clear: The student disagrees with the curfew. The student maintains the focus of the paper by using well-developed paragraphs, as in paragraph 2, where the student begins with the statement (*There are many problems with this statement*) and gives several examples of these problems (*violence does not take place in a community only at night, drugs are a problem in every community and do not discriminate against any type of student or time of day*). The student uses counterarguments in paragraphs 2 and 3 to logically refute the opposition's opinion. The student uses transitions to smoothly join the paragraphs and examples together (*A curfew like this would also, Obviously, According to supporters*). The details and examples in the body paragraphs show that the student has carefully planned the argument. In addition to good content and organization, the essay uses strong vocabulary (*flaws, scandalize, lurking*). The sentences are varied and interesting, and there are few, if any, grammatical errors.

Model Score 5

To try to reduce juvenile violence and crime, many towns have chosen to enforce curfews on minors under the age of 18. People who support these curfews believe they would lower community problems such as violence, graffiti, and drugs. People who oppose curfews for minors claim that these curfews stereotype minors by assuming that citizens under the age of 18 are the only people who commit crimes. I actually think a curfew would be a good idea. A curfew in our community would make the community a safer, cleaner place and would help build stronger families.

Many teens get into a lot of trouble late at night. They are out late hanging around doing very little that is constructive. Teens who are out past 10:00 p.m. are more likely to drink alcohol, experiment with drugs, and commit crimes such as vandalism and robbery. It's too hard for teens to resist peer pressure when it's late and they are sleep-deprived. A curfew would ensure that most teens are safely in there homes late at night. This way the teens themselves are safer from peer-pressure and other community members are safe from teens who might do terrible things while sleep-deprived or under the influence of drugs and alcohol. It's true that not every crime is committed by a teenager, but if we can eliminate some crime with this curfew, it allows the police to concentrate on other people committing crimes. Either way, crime is reduced and the community us safer.

You may notice that teens are not the neatest people in the world. Most teens rooms are a disaster area. Teens who are permitted to wander aimlessly around the neighborhood tend to create a mess. Even if they are not drinking alcohol, teens gathering in a park or parking lot will tend to leave cans, food wrappers, and sometimes cigarette butts all over the place. Some teens deliberately cause a mess by overturning garbage cans, spray painting on buildings and fences, or breaking windows. Of course, most teens are going to wait until the cover of night to do this, so having a curfew would eliminate these problems.

Finally, having a curfew would help build stronger families. Many teens go out and stay out all night long. They never interact with their parents or siblings. They think a night at home will be boring. But a curfew like this would force teens to stay home with their families. At first it may seem like torture, but if parents take advantage of it and create a warm, loving, fun home environment, teens will enjoy staying home and families will become stronger. Without the curfew, it's too difficult for parents to force their teens to stay at home; it becomes a source of arguments. If there were a curfew, the parents could "blame" it on the law. That way it doesn't feel so much like the parents are harassing the teenager.

I think a curfew is a good idea. As a teenager myself I see the trouble teens get into late at night. I have a good time when I stay home with my family and I'd like to see other teens have this experience too.

Critique

This essay shows a good understanding of the prompt and shows some insight into the complexities of this issue. The essay has a clear thesis statement. The essay contains specific examples to support the thesis, showing how teenagers get into trouble late at night, and contains a counterargument in paragraph 2. Overall, the essay is generally well organized; it uses clear logic with good transitions between ideas. The essay shows good command of written English with attempts at varying sentence structure and attempts at sophisticated vocabulary use that may not be as successful as the model score 6.

Model Score 4

Curfews for minors are a bad idea. Curfews make it illegal for minors to be out in public between the hours of 10 PM and 5 AM. These curfews are a bad idea for several reasons. If a minor is out after 10 PM, it does not mean that this minor is comiting a crime. People over the age of 18 commit crimes too. Sometimes it is necessary for a minor to be out after 10 PM for work and for friends. Also, just because a minor is out after 10 PM doesn't mean he's a bad kid. He shouldn't get in trouble for not really doing anything bad.

The people who want to create a curfew think that it'll create less crime in the community. It might do that with some kids, sure, but it won't stop crime all together. If a kid knows he has to be in by 10 PM he might decide not to write graffiti on the walls or hang out and do drugs, but that doesn't mean that other people won't. Old people commit crimes too. Also, a kid can do drugs after school at a friends house. He doesn't have to do it at night. He can draw or write on the sides of buildings before 10 PM too. In the wintertime, it is dark outside at 7 PM. Kids will do the same things, they will just do them earlier in the day.

Sometimes, too, a minor needs to be out after 10 PM. For example a kid might have a job that doesn't get out until 10 PM and than the kid needs to drive home. If he gets caught driving, he could get in trouble. Or what if he is at a friends house and they are just having a fun time or doing there home-work, not doing anything wrong or anything, but just hanging out. If he for-gets what time it is and he leaves a little too late he could get in trouble. That is not fair if he is a good kid.

This brings me to my last point. If a minor gets in trouble for staying out after the curfew it could ruin his reputation. He might be a good student who wants to get a scholarship to college. He can't get a scholarship with a police record. He was probably out late studying anyway if he's a smart kid. Maybe the people who create these curfews could make some guidelines to follow so that kids could stay out later if there is a special event or for work or study-ing. That would make it easier to follow and good kids wouldn't get in trouble.

In conclusion, I think that curfews are a bad idea. They don't change any-thing and don't make kids stop doing inapropriate things.

Critique

This essay is an adequate response. In the opening, the student states the main idea of the essay: *Curfews for minors are a bad idea.* The student then briefly outlines the content of the essay. The student continues the focus throughout the essay, staying with the position of dis-agreeing with the curfew legislation, and develops the essay by attempting to give three dis-tinct reasons. However, paragraphs 3 and 4 are quite similar and possibly could have been discussed in one paragraph. The student does attempt transitions between both sentences and paragraphs (*For example, Sometimes, too, This brings me to my last point*). Although this helps the organization of the essay, it does little to add to the development of the paragraphs, which is weak. Paragraph 2 gives several details to support the student's opinion that cur-fews do not lessen crime in a community (*Old people commit crimes too, a kid can do drugs after school, Kids will do the same things, they will just do them earlier in the day*). However, paragraph 4 lacks solid details or examples to support the student's idea that a curfew could ruin a minor's reputation. There is only one sketchy detail (*He can't get a scholarship with a police record*). This uneven development hinders the effectiveness of the essay.

The student uses basic vocabulary and sentences, and makes several spelling and grammatical errors (*scholership, just having a fun time or doing there homework, at a friends house*), but they do not interfere with the meaning of the essay.

Model Score 3

I'm getting very tired of adults not trusting teenagers. This curfew idea just adds to the problem. It's a terrible idea.

People who want this curfew think that all teenagers are out to vandelize and cause trouble. That's not true. Some teens are trouble-makers but most aren't. Most teens are good kids. They want to go out at night to have fun, not cause trouble. If we had a curfew teens would probably not be able to have much fun. They would have to go in their houses so early that they wouldn't be able to really do anything. The curfew might keep the bad teens from doing bad things but it punnishes the good teens at the same time and that's not fair.

The curfew would make it pratically immpossible for teens to have jobs and that also wouldn't be fair. Teens can't really get a job at McDonalds if they can't work passed 10:00pm.

The whole problem is that adults don't trust teens and they should. Most teens are fine. Maybe only teens that have been bad should have the curfew instead of everyone.

Critique

This essay shows developing skill. The writer shows a clear understanding of the assignment and takes a clear stand on the issue. The essay lacks adequate development, however. The ideas are very general and somewhat repetitive: *Some teens are trouble-makers but most aren't. Most teens are good kids. They want to go out at night to have fun, not cause trouble.* The essay has an adequate organization but lacks strong transitions between ideas. The essay shows some control of written language but makes some obvious spelling errors (*vandelize, punnishes*) and lacks sophistication.

Model Score 2

A curfew is when there is a time limit on when you can go out. Sometimes a curfew can be good or bad.

Its bad to have a curfew when you want to do something fun like go to a movie or out with friends. But a curfew could be good if it keeps you out of trouble, like if your drinking or something then youd have to stop because of the curfew.

People think teens do bad things when their out late at night and sometimes their right, but ususaly teens are just hanging out and that's not that bad.

I think a curfew might be a good idea in bad arreas of town, but I would-n't want to have a curfew even though I don't do bad things.

Critique

This essay shows a weak understanding of the prompt. The writer does not take a clear stand on the issue and offers no counterarguments. There are no transitions between ideas, and the ideas themselves are vague and confusing. It's difficult to tell whether the writer is for or against the curfew. The essay contains a number of grammatical and spelling errors that show a poor grasp of written language.

Model Score 1

I dont think that kids are crimanales. My mom lets me stay out late and im not a crimanale. I dont do drugs.

sometimes policeman chais 14 yearolds down the street on tv butt I dont see that in my town becawse they dont. besids, 14 yearolds get privleges. it says so in that adendmint.

if you play your stero loud at night you might comit a crim because it is a minor but the police shud not chais you becawse of privleges.

no one shud inforce laws on kids who are not crimanales.

Critique

This essay shows little to no understanding of the prompt. The student confused much of the information. For example, the student confused the Fourteenth Amendment with 14-year-olds. The random and inappropriate details (*sometimes policeman chais 14 yearolds down the street*) weaken the attempt made by the student to establish the main idea stated in paragraph 1. The student writes about very few, if any, outside details. The student also makes severe grammatical errors that take away from the meaning of the essay and make it quite difficult to read (*crimanales, adendmint*).

▶ Sample Answers to Prompt #15

Model Score 6

Picture your beloved pet—a dog, cat, bird, or hamster—being killed, then shipped to one of thousands of schools to be dissected by students, many of whom are just taking the course for credit and who have no real interest in learning about health or biology. Now picture an unknown animal. Does the fact that the animal wasn't someone's pet make it any different? Your pet has emotions; it shows love, loyalty, fear, and pain. Obviously, these attributes are not unique to animals that are pets. All animals have these feelings. That is why using any animal for dissection is cruel, a violation of the animals' rights, and completely unnecessary.

The use of animals for dissection in schools is cruel. No matter how "humanely" the animals are put to death, they are still losing their lives. Some of them lose their lives quite young—before they even have a chance to live. Some schools use piglets as dissection animals in classes. Beyond that, some of these animals are specifically bred for dissection purposes. They live their lives in cages basically only being provided the bare necessities until they are put to sleep. Not only does this make their death cruel; it makes their lives cruel as well.

Animals have rights. Just like humans, animals have the right to live their lives and pursue happiness. Many animals enjoy their lives. You can tell when an animal is happy. Whether it be a dog that runs and plays and wags its tail, a cat that contentedly curls up on your lap, a horse that prances in the field, or a bird that sings—all animals show their enjoyment of life. We have no right to take that life away just because we are bigger or stronger or have more power than they do. This is the worst form of bullying. Opponents to this idea cite survival of the fittest or the biblical tradition of having dominion over the earth to support the use of animals in this way. However, simply because humans have advanced technological knowledge does not necessarily mean that the human species is morally or emotionally better than other animals. There-fore, we should not simply use animals for our purposes.

Finally, the use of animals for dissection in school classes is completely unnecessary. Because we as humans have advanced knowledge of technology, we should use it. It is now entirely possible to re-create the internal and exter-nal images of animals (and humans) via computer technology. Rather than continuing to take the lives of innocent animals, students should use the infor-mation already gained and catalogued in computer programs to study science issues. Not only does this save the lives of animals, it is probably safer for students because now they do not have to be concerned with contracting a dis-ease while dissecting an infected animal.

We have been destroying animals for our own selfish purposes long enough. It's time to use the brains we were given (or have developed) to make the world a better place for all its inhabitants, not just humans.

Critique

This essay shows an excellent and insightful understanding of the prompt. The student takes a clear stand on the issue and uses specific details and examples (explaining how animals enjoy their lives) to support the thesis. The student provides a counterargument in paragraph 3: *However, simply because humans have advanced technological knowledge does not necessarily mean that the human species is morally or emotionally better than other animals.* In the fourth paragraph, the student provides a strong argument combined with a solution to the problem (using computer-generated images). The essay is well organized with good use of transitions. The essay shows a strong command of written language and contains virtually no grammatical errors while showing sophisticated vocabulary and varied sentence structure.

Model Score 5

What's more important—animals or humans? The students on campus who are crying out against the use of animals for dissection in science classes obviously think animals are more important. This is a nice sentiment, but what will those same students say when someone in their family contracts an illness and a trial drug to cure the illness needs to be tested on an animal? Then they might have a different story. I believe that we should continue to use animals in science classes.

First of all, using animals for dissection is not cruel. People believe that animals feel the same way about death as humans do. I disagree. Maybe animals show emotion or maybe we just think they show emotions. Animal behaviorists have a difficult time figuring out how much emotion animals have as opposed to how much we just perceive. Either way, animals just do not have the higher thinking power to worry about death the way we do. As long as they are put to death humanely, I don't think the animals even understand that they are dying. They just feel very sleepy.

Another argument these student activists have is that the animals are bred for dissection and don't have fulfilling lives. Again, I don't think animals have the higher order of thinking to worry about whether or not their lives have been fulfilled. Because it would be dangerous to use a diseased animal in a class dissection, the animals we dissect are healthy and usually adult. So they have lived their lives, and they have been well-cared for or they wouldn't be healthy. And the bottom line again is, I don't think the animals even know any better.

Finally, it is necessary to use animals for dissection in science classes. Students learn a great deal by studying real organs and tissues. Some of these students will eventually go on to become doctors or researchers who will eventually save people's lives. I think the sacrifice of a frog, rat, or pig is well worth that. I don't think reading or looking at pictures in a book has the same educational value or will spark the same passion in students to advance their scientific education and careers.

Ultimately, there are more important things in the world to protest than whether or not a rat or a frog winds up on a dissection table. Students should put their energies into more worthwhile causes—causes that will help humankind, the way animal dissection ultimately does.

Critique

This essay shows a good understanding of the prompt and offers some specific arguments to support the idea that animals should be used for dissection. The indirect thesis statement is a bit weak, but it clearly states the writer's point of view. The essay uses logical arguments and contains counterarguments in paragraphs 2 and 3. The essay shows a good command of written language but lacks the style and sophistication of a model score 6 essay.

Model Score 4

I have been brought up to believe that all life is precious and that the life of an animal is not to be taken unless it's for a very good reason. I love all animals and I am very upset about the animal dissections that occur in science classes. I think this is cruel both for the animals and for the students.

Dissecting an animal is cruel for the animal itself. Even though the animals are already dead when they are dissected, I still think the whole process is cruel. The poor animals that are used in science class are bred just for dissection purposes. It's like they don't even have a real life. As soon as they're big and old enough, they are killed and shipped to schools for dissection. Even the dissection is cruel. Sure the animal is dead, but now instead of being able to just rest in peace, the poor thing is cut up and all its parts are taken out. Think about your favorite pet. Would you like it if your cat or dog died and then someone came in and started cutting it all apart?

The whole process of dissection is also cruel for students. Some students actually get sick from the smell and from having to handle the insides of an animal. I've been in classes where students had to stop dissecting because they felt faint and nauseas. Emotionally, it is hard on some students to have to deal with death. They see something that was once alive, and it is now dead. It reminds them of pets or even people who have died. This can be very upsetting to some students.

There are also other students like me who simply become upset when they think about how these animals died for no reason. Some students may even have moral or religious ideas that state that killing a living thing is wrong. The school should not force these students to go against their beliefs by making them handle a dead animal.

School should be an enjoyable place for students to learn. Cutting up animals makes school an uncomfortable place and a place that brings up a lot of bad feelings in some students. School should be a place where values are supported, especially the value of life.

Critique

This essay shows a good understanding of the assignment. The thesis statement is clear and fairly well supported in the body of the essay with details and examples although some ideas in paragraphs 3 and 4 are a bit repetitive. The essay contains a weak attempt at a counterargument in paragraph 2: *Even though the animals are already dead when they are dissected, I still think the whole process is cruel.* The arguments against dissection of animals are logical. This essay is well organized overall, with each body paragraph developing an idea to support the thesis that dissection is cruel for animals and students. The essay shows an adequate command of written language but lacks sophistication in vocabulary use and sentence structure.

Model Score 3

There are some students in this school who refuse to dissect animals. They say they feel sorry for the animals. I think they are wrong. Dissecting animals is part of what we have to do for our grade, and the animals are allready dead so they don't know what's going on.

Dissecting animals gives us the chance to see some really cool things. Seeing stuff in a book is not the same as seeing it in real life. Its important for students to have experiances like this in life. We will learn and remember stuff better if we see it and do it for ourselves. Learning about pigs or frogs will help us learn more about ourselves and how our body works.

Another thing is that the animals are dead allready, so we don't have to kill them. They do it in a humane way, which means the animals do not feel anything, they just die. Once their dead, they don't feel anything, so cutting them up is not a problem. Plus, its not like were just going to hack them to pieces. We are going to carefully cut and remove some of the organs. You could think of it as the animals are doing a good thing in their life by helping us learn.

I don't feel sorry for the animals. That's part of what their there for, to help students learn. I think dissecting them is fine and students should'nt worry so much about the animals.

Critique

This essay shows an adequate understanding of the assignment. The thesis statement is a bit weak: *Dissecting animals is part of what we have to do for our grade, and the animals are already dead so they don't know what's going on.* However, the rest of the essay supports it pretty well with some logical arguments. The essay would have been stronger with better organization and better development using specific examples. The essay is a bit repetitive in paragraphs 1 and 3. This essay contains a weak counterargument in paragraph 4: *Plus, its not like were just going to hack them to pieces. We are going to carefully cut and remove some of the organs.* The essay shows some command of written language but contains some simplistic sentences with simple vocabulary (*Seeing stuff in a book is not the same as seeing it in real life, Another thing is that*) and some awkward sentences (*That's part of what their there for, to help students learn*). There are some spelling, grammar, and punctuation errors, but they do not make the composition very difficult to read or understand.

Model Score 2

Some people think dissecting animals in class is wrong, others don't care. I don't like to dissect animals but I don't think it's really wrong either.

Animals can be pets or they can be like lab rats. You wouldn't want to dissect a pet, but its ok to dissect a lab rat. A pet gives you love and companionship. You would be upset if it died. A lab rat is just a thing in a cage. Its purpose is bassically to get dissected.

As long as the animal was ment to be dissected I don't have a problem with it. But I wouldn't want to see Fifi on my lab table.

Critique

This essay shows a very weak understanding of the prompt. The writer does not take a clear stand on the issue, as shown in the weak thesis statement. The essay drifts a bit off track by focusing on the differences between pets and lab animals. It is undeveloped and shows a weak command of written language as evidenced by grammatical and spelling errors.

Model Score 1

I do not want to dissect animals in sience class. I think it is grose and mean. Animals are living things with a life too and we wouldn't want to be cut up so why should we do it to them.

If I have to cut a frog or a pig I will probally get sick. I will have to leave class and not come back until its done. I think frogs and pigs are cute and I will get very sad to have to cut it up. We did a worm once and I even fealt bad about that. Also the smell. It is grose and makes me sick.

Please don't let us have to dissect animals. We can just look at a picture and that's it.

Critique

This essay shows a poor understanding of the assignment. The writer makes it clear that he or she does not want to dissect an animal but does not give logical arguments against animal dissection as a school policy. There is no clear thesis statement; therefore, the body paragraph does not really support a particular belief. It simply explains what will happen if the writer has to dissect an animal. The essay is not developed enough to show an overall organizational pattern, but the paragraphs themselves lack strong organization. For example, paragraph 2 deals with several different topics at once, without developing any one of them. The language used shows a weak command of written language with simplistic sentence structure and simple vocabulary. There are spelling, grammar, and punctuation errors that sometimes make the composition difficult to read and understand.

▶ Sample Answers to Prompt #25

Model Score 6

When the founding fathers of our Constitution included the Bill of Rights, they wanted to guarantee American citizens the right to free speech. Although freedom of speech is a valuable right of all American citizens, it has been abused by those who are manipulating the Constitution and its writers' intent so that they may gain fame, wealth, or attention. The only way to amend this problem is to impose censorship on these abusers. Unfortunately, the Internet has become a hotbed of abuse of free speech and needs to be censored, especially in our schools so that students are protected, education continues, and the authors of the offensive websites will eventually shut down their sites.

Use of the Internet in school has skyrocketed in past few years. It has opened a door to an aspect of education never dreamed of before. Students and teachers can use the Internet for research, demonstration, and to learn and practice new skills. However, these benefits can only occur when the Internet is used wisely. Of all the websites available through the World Wide Web, only a small percentage is really worthwhile. Many others simply use the web to exercise their warped version of free speech. Students must be protected from this abuse. Some students who are curious purposely go to questionable websites. Once there they find it difficult to turn away. As humans, we have a natural inclination toward the bizarre and even salacious. That's why it's up to schools to protect their students from themselves—and their natural curiosity— by imposing restrictions on the Internet. Other students innocently type a word into a search engine and are directed to an offensive website. It is well known that certain violent and sexual images become imprinted on the brain and are nearly impossible to eradicate. Again, schools should protect their students from exposure to a potential long-lasting horror.

Another reason schools should have tight control over the Internet is to ensure that education continues uninterrupted. It's too easy to become side-tracked by intriguing, but unhealthy, websites and games. Yes, people should exercise some self-control, but if the school is in the business of education, it should make sure that all of its accoutrements enhance education, not distract from it. It's a waste of time and energy for school administrators to try to hunt down Internet abusers. That time and energy can be saved if the school has only an Intranet with preapproved sites. Schools should be educating students, not policing them.

Finally, if more schools make the decision to curb Internet access, maybe the people who create these offensive sites will be shut down. Most of these people make money off advertising on their websites. They promise advertisers that many people view their websites. If a large percentage of computer users were suddenly not included in that calculation, maybe these abusers would find better uses of their time and talents.

An Intranet is a great solution to the problem of Internet abuse. It allows students quick and easy access to preapproved, educational material. But it protects students from people who do not really understand the idea behind freedom of speech. "Censorship" is not a dirty word; it is a way to ensure that people do not abuse the right of free speech and make life more difficult for others.

Critique

This essay shows an excellent understanding of the assignment. It includes interesting ideas and insightful treatment of personal observations in connection with the assignment. The thesis statement is strong and clear. The essay contains strong supporting details that are well developed and explained throughout the essay, including three strong and logical reasons for the establishment of an Intranet in the school. The essay is well organized with paragraphs appropriately broken out and good transitions between ideas. The essay remains focused and on topic throughout. The language used is highly sophisticated, and the essay contains few, if any, spelling, grammar, or capitalization errors.

Model Score 5

Members of the community are considering limiting Internet access in the schools. They believe that young people are at risk of being exposed to inappropriate material on the Internet. I disagree with this proposal for a variety of reasons.

The Internet contains a wealth of information for students. It is a valuable educational and resource tool. By using the Internet students can "visit" great places like museums and government offices. Students can get the very latest, up-to-date information on science, health, and world events. To cut students off from this wealth would be a great disservice to them. While it's true that many websites are offensive and inappropriate, most are not. We should not "throw out the baby with the bathwater" by completely eliminating student access to the World Wide Web.

There are some students who purposely investigate questionable websites. These students are usually just curious or they may be chronic offenders who need to be dealt with. However, it would be very easy to figure out who these students are and limit their access to the Internet. If every student had his or her own password and login name, this problem would be eliminated. We shouldn't punish all students for the actions of a few. Censoring the entire Internet from all students just because a few can't control themselves is a violation of the students' rights.

I think an Intranet will be too limiting to be useful to students. It will take too much time and effort to research websites and then upload them one by one once they have approval. Plus doing this will cause all students doing research to have the same information from the same source. We might as well just all copy off one another and then there would be even more trouble! The point is, what's the use of doing research if we're all going to look in exactly the same place for information? The idea behind research is to find new, interesting ideas and information.

Replacing the Internet with an Intranet is a bad idea. It will be too limiting and cumbersome and there are better ways to deal with the problem of inappropriate websites.

Critique

This essay shows a good understanding of the prompt and offers some specific arguments to support the idea that an Intranet should not replace the Internet. The indirect thesis statement is a bit weak, but it clearly states the writer's point of view. The essay uses logical arguments and contains counterarguments in paragraphs 2 and 3. The essay shows a good command of written language but lacks the style and sophistication of a Model Score 6 essay.

Model Score 4

Censorship is when anything that is considered offensive or harmful is limited so that people cannot have access to it. For some people that includes many things from realistic video games to certain types of music. I think censorship is not a good idea in America because that's part of what we fought for—freedom. Many people think the Internet should be under censorship, but I don't agree.

Because it was invented, the Internet has been a great thing for many people. I enjoy doing research for school on it. There are many websites that have great information on them. I especially like to go on websites that deal with science and health. But some people think the Internet should be censored. They think students will go on Internet sites that are violent or have improper content on them. Its true that some students may go to these sites. But most students don't. Also, if you censor the Internet who will decide what gets censored and what doesn't. There are things on the Internet that are fine for older students but not for younger ones.

The problem with censorship is that it means different things to everybody. I don't think there should be pornography or super violent stuff on the Internet. But I do think some stuff is ok even if it may have some questionable things on it. For example, a health website may have a picture or drawing of a naked person, but that's not pornography. Or a website about war may have violent images on it, but that's what war is about, and you can't really censor it or you don't have the truth.

I think that everyone needs to decide what is a problem for themselves and censor his own Internet instead of having the school do it. This will help teach students responsibility and make it so that all students don't have to pay for the actions of a few. Make students sign an agreement that they will not abuse the Internet at the school. A good compromise might be to block some obviously non-educational websites.

Critique

This essay shows a good understanding of the assignment. The writer takes a clear stand on the issue even though the thesis statement is a bit weak and undeveloped. This essay is well organized overall with some specific examples, but again, it lacks some development.

The essay shows an adequate command of written language but lacks sophistication in vocabulary use and sentence structure.

Model Score 3

The school board is thinking about cutting off the Internet and going to an Intranet at the school. I think this is probably a good idea.

A lot of students waste time on the school computers. They say their doing research but their really just fooling around. They may not be playing games or anything, but they go to websites that have pretty much nothing to do with school or anything educational.

If we had an Intranet we could still use the computers for research and stuff but it would be for students who are serious about it, not students who just want to waste time. Anyone who wanted to do more research outside of school could do it at home or at the public library.

School is a place for learning and not fooling around on the Internet all day. The Intranet would avoid this problem and make it so that real students could do their work and the people who don't really want to use the computer seriously will think it's boring and not take up all the computers.

Critique

This essay shows an adequate understanding of the assignment. The thesis statement is a bit weak: *I think this is probably a good idea.* The rest of the essay, however, supports the thesis with some logical arguments. The essay would have been stronger with better organization and better development using specific examples. The essay shows some command of written language but contains some simplistic sentences with simple vocabulary and some awkward sentences. There are some spelling, grammar, and punctuation errors, but they do not make the composition very difficult to read or understand.

Model Score 2

Censoring the Internet at school is just another way for the school to control us. The school doesn't want people going on the Internet and seeing a bunch of stuff that they think is bad for us.

The problem is that the school thinks it knows everything about how to get us to learn things. They don't realize that the Internet is probably the most used thing that students have to learn. A lot of students who don't really learn that much in class because the books and teachers are boring will learn more on the Internet.

So what if sometimes you see something that's supposebly not appropriate. Who cares. Its not like its really anything new, most people see all that junk on tv anyway.

Leave the Internet in the schools, it's the best thing about them, I probably wouldn't even go if we didn't have computers.

Critique

This essay shows a very weak understanding of the prompt. The writer does take a stand on the issue, but the support for it is weak and repetitive. The introduction does not contain a thesis statement at all. The essay drifts a bit off track by focusing on how students learn more from the Internet than from books and teachers. It is undeveloped and shows a weak command of written language, as evidenced by the grammatical and spelling errors.

Model Score 1

Censorship is when peple wont let you see or watch things that they think are bad for you. Like the Internet, the school doesn't want us to have the Internet cause people are looking at things that they shouldn't be.

It really doesn't matter to me what the school does with the computers cause i have one at home I use and I can just go on that one and do stuff. Most students have the same thing, so the school probally shouldn't even bother doing anything cause the students will just go on the sites at home anyways.

Critique

This essay shows a lack of understanding with regard to the assignment. The student shows some understanding about censorship, but does not take a clear stand on the issue in the prompt and does not develop the essay with specific examples. The essay drifts off topic by repeatedly stating that students can use the Internet at home. The essay is poorly developed and lacks a logical form of organization. The language used shows a serious lack of command of written language, and there are numerous spelling, grammar, punctuation, and capitalization errors.

▶ Sample Answers for Prompt #35

Model Score 6

Obesity has become a major problem in the United States. This health problem leads to other serious issues such as heart disease and diabetes. The school board is considering a plan to help students fight this problem. The new lunch program based on nutritious food and the elimination of soda machines is necessary for students to obtain nutritious food and the program will help students become healthier, more energetic, and even smarter.

Many students in our schools have a weight problem. More and more children and teenagers are battling obesity than ever before. Much of this is due to poor food choices. At home, many families have two parents who work or even just one parent who works two jobs. This leaves little time for shopping for and preparing nutritious meals. It's simply quicker and easier to go to a fast-food restaurant or throw some macaroni and cheese into the microwave than to prepare a well-balanced meal. That's where the school comes in. At least the school can provide students with a nutritious lunch. It may be the only really nutritious food the students get. While there might be some resistance at first, students will eventually begin to eat and enjoy the new food. If students become hungry enough, they'll try it and find that they actually like it. They will begin to feel and look better. The soda machines do provide money for the school, but is the money worth the health of the students? Additionally, if we replace the soda vending machines with water vending machines, we will still make some money.

Eating healthy lunches will help students have more energy throughout the day. Students and teachers complain that many students tend to crash during the early afternoon classes. This is usually because students have eaten a lunch high in sugar and carbohydrates. This type of food gives a quick burst of energy, which the student typically uses up during the period itself, and then causes a rapid decline of energy, causing the student to feel sluggish and sleepy. Nutritious food would eliminate this problem. If students eat a meal of protein, whole grains, and vegetables, they will have a more steady supply of energy to keep them going throughout the day. Some opponents say that many students will boycott the new lunch program and not eat lunch at all, making them tired during the day. This may happen a few times, but most teenagers do not like the feeling of being hungry and tired. They will eventually begin to eat the food, even if it's just one part of the lunch that they like.

Finally, this new lunch program will actually help students increase their academic performance. Healthy food makes people feel better and perform with more energy and alertness. This means students will pay more attention in class, have more energy to do required work, and think more clearly and creatively. This can only lead to better grades and better test scores, something students and teachers alike are always pursuing.

The new lunch program may intimidate some students. People are creatures of habit and are initially resistant to change of any kind. But much of eating is an acquired taste for certain foods. While students may miss their tacos and chocolate chip cookies, they will eventually come to appreciate and hopefully prefer grilled chicken and a nice juicy apple.

Critique

This essay shows an excellent and insightful understanding of the prompt. The writer takes a clear stand on the issue with a strong, direct thesis statement: *The new lunch program based on nutritious food and the elimination of soda machines is necessary for students to obtain nutritious food and the program will help students become healthier, more energetic, and even smarter.* The essay is well developed with specific examples, reasons, and sound logic. It contains two counterarguments in paragraphs 2 and 3, stating that money from the soda machines should not take precedence over student heath and that students who boycott the lunches will eventually begin to eat them. The essay shows excellent command of written language with sophisticated vocabulary and varied sentence structure.

Model Score 5

School cafeterias are not well known for gourmet food, but over the years, they've gotten better at knowing what teenagers like to eat. Now the school wants to change all that by starting a new lunch program with nutritious food and eliminating the soda machines. Doing this will actually harm the students and waste a lot of money.

Lunch is one of the most important parts of a student's day at school. It's a time when students can relax and have fun. Part of that fun is enjoying the food. Students have their likes and dislikes, but usually there's something they will eat, even if it's just the packages of chocolate chip cookies that everyone likes so much. The point is to have something in the middle of the day that will give students some energy to make it through the rest of the day. It doesn't need to be a full meal of chicken, vegetables, and whole-grain rolls. Teenagers are picky about their food and they are also a little rebellious. If the school only offers food that many teens don't like, they just won't eat it. Then many students will be trying to make it through the day without lunch. Many students do not eat breakfast, so now they will have missed two meals. This could lead to students fainting or losing a lot of weight, which could also be dangerous. If the students do eat the full meals presented in the cafeteria, this could also be a problem. The lunches we have now are light food—sandwiches, tacos. If students eat a full meal and then go right out to play gym, they could get sick.

Having a program like this will also waste a lot of money. We all know that better food costs more money to buy and takes more skill to prepare. The school will have to increase its food budget and possibly hire different people to prepare the food. All this money will go to waste because most of the students won't eat the food. Burgers and tacos may not be the healthiest foods but they also don't cost very much and teenagers will actually eat it. Eliminating the soda machines will also cost the school a lot of money. The money from those machines goes toward school supplies that benefit the students. So once again, if we have this new lunch program students are being harmed. Yes, we could replace the soda machines with water machines, but they will definitely not generate as much income and students will have to sacrifice things such as sports equipment, uniforms, or art supplies.

People will say that the school has a responsibility to provide nutritious food for the students. First of all, burgers and tacos do have nutrition; it's not like students are eating nothing but candy for lunch. Secondly, we're only talking about one meal a day; many students get very nutritious food at home. One meal is not going to make that much difference.

This new lunch program could do more harm than good. I appreciate the school trying to make students healthier, but that really is a personal choice and the responsibility of students and their parents. The school should concentrate on educating students, not trying to change their diets.

Critique

This essay shows a good understanding of the prompt, and the writer takes a strong stand on the issue. The essay is well developed with the exception of paragraph 4, which contains only a counterargument and could have been developed a bit more to make the essay more balanced. The essay gives specific examples and is logically sound. The writing shows a strong command of written language but lacks some of the sophistication of the model score 6 essay.

Model Score 4

To try to fight obesity and make students more healthy, the school board is thinking about changing the cafeteria menu to get rid of the junk food and have only low-fat meals and snacks. They are also thinking about getting rid of the soda machines. I think this is a good idea.

Teenagers eat way too much junk. Most of my friends don't eat breakfast or if they do, it's a doughnut or sugared cereal. Then when lunch time comes they eat a package of cookies and a soda. It's actually kind of gross. This program would force students to eat better. I know if I have a choice, I'll eat the less healthy food because I think it tastes better. But if all I had was healthy choices, I'd be eating better. I'd also probably lose some weight and so would other people. Most people I know do need to lose some weight. Some people think that the students won't eat this food, but that's not really a problem. If the teenager is overweight, skipping a meal might not be a bad idea.

Getting rid of the soda machines is also a good idea. I know the school makes some money off of them so losing the money would be bad, but not having soda around all the time would be more healthy. I had three cavities last year and I think it's mostly because I drink so much soda.

I definitely think a healthier lunch program is a good idea. It may take some getting used too but I think it will be better for everyone in the long run.

Critique

This essay shows a good understanding of the prompt, and the writer takes a strong stand on the issue. The introduction is somewhat of a restatement of the prompt, but it works. The essay lacks some development. It's only four paragraphs in length, and the writer focused a bit too much on personal issues related to the issue (cavities due to drinking soda). The writing shows a good command of written language but lacks sophistication.

Model Score 3

The school board is considering changing the school lunch program so that all the food is low-fat. They are also interested in getting rid of all the soda machines. I think this is a terrible idea.

No one likes low-fat food, especially teenagers. We like to eat junk food. We have to eat enough healthy food at home, we don't need it pushed on us at school. Actually I don't even think the food at school is that unhealthy. It's not like it's fast food or anything. OK, there's burgers, but their not all greasy or anything. If we get low fat food no one will eat it. No one wants to eat whole grain pitas with tuna in them. I've tried low-fat cookies and they were terrible They tasted like cardboard.

As far as getting rid of the soda machines, that will cause a big problem. We all like to drink soda. It's refreshing and picks us up in the afternoons. Also the soda machines make money for the school. We get supplies and stuff from that money. I think the students will probably rebel if we get rid of the soda machines or you'll have a bunch of people cutting just to get to the store to buy some soda.

This program is a bad idea. I wouldn't put it in, but if you do watch out because the students and probably even some teachers are not going to like it.

Critique

This essay shows a basic understanding of the prompt, and the writer takes a clear stand on the issue. It is undeveloped, as it is only four paragraphs. This essay focuses on the writer's personal dislike of eating healthy foods, as well as what will happen if the plan is implemented, rather than citing specific, logical reasons for not implementing the plan. The writing shows some command of written language, but it is very casual and unsophisticated.

Model Score 2

I think the school should maybe go into a healthier lunch plan. I also think that the soda machines should also be out.

The soda machines never work anyway. I loose so much money in them. Or if I don't loose the money I get the wrong soda. So I don't care if those go away.

The lunches are pretty bad. All we eat is hamburgers, tacos and some kids only eat chips and cookies for lunch. Thats pretty bad and I can see that a lot of people need to loose weight too. The new lunch plan might help people eat better and loose weight.

But it would be hard to always eat healthy food. Everyone likes a treat once in awhile so maybe a totally healthy lunch might not be so great.

Critique

This essay shows a weak understanding of the prompt. It does not take a very clear stand on the issue because, although the writer makes a clear statement about wanting the new lunch program in the introduction, the writer drifts off focus by discussing the fact that he or she loses money in the soda machines. In addition, in the conclusion, the writer says that the new program *might not be so great*. The essay is very undeveloped and lacks logical reasoning. The writing shows some grasp of written language, but it is very unsophisticated and contains spelling and grammatical errors that make some of the essay difficult to understand.

Model Score 1

There are good and bad things about the new lunch plan. Its always a good idear to eat better but ususually its not that fun. So the school should think about it before they do it.

Most kids and adults like soda. No one really likes to drink water, but they will if that's all there is so if the soda machines go out and theres only water that would be good. But if you do that the water fountians need fixing theyre always broken or actually its kind of dirty so maybe we should not use them and just go back to the soda machine.

Im not really shure what the best thing is. Well the best thing is to eat healthy and not drink soda but whose really gonna do that.

Critique

This essay shows a lack of understanding of the prompt and does not take a stand on the issue at all. The body of the essay drifts off topic by focusing on the condition of the water fountains. The writer admits in the conclusion that he's not sure what to think of the issue. The writing shows a poor grasp of written language, and there are many spelling and grammatical errors that make much of the essay difficult to understand.

Notes

Notes

Notes

Notes

Notes

Notes

Notes

Notes

Notes

Notes

Special FREE Offer from LearningExpress

LearningExpress will help you succeed on the ACT Writing Test

 Go to the LearningExpress Practice Center at www.Learning ExpressFreeOffer.com, an interactive online resource exclusively for LearningExpress customers.

Now that you've purchased LearningExpress's *ACT Essay Practice: Write Here, Write Now!*, you have **FREE** access to:

- **Writing practice exercises** and **an instantly scored ACT practice essay** to help you improve your writing score
- Strengthen your writing skills and focus your study with our **customized diagnostic reports**

Follow the simple instructions on the scratch card in your copy of *ACT Essay Practice: Write Here, Write Now!*. Use your individualized access code found on the scratch card and go to www.LearningExpressFreeOffer.com to sign in. Start practicing online for the ACT Writing Test right away!

Once you've logged on, use the spaces below to write in your access code and newly created password for easy reference:

Access Code: _____   Password: _____

Nokomis Public Library